OECD Series on Carbon Pricing and Energy Taxation

Pricing Greenhouse Gas Emissions 2024

GEARING UP TO BRING EMISSIONS DOWN

OECD
BETTER POLICIES FOR BETTER LIVES

This document, as well as any data and map included herein, are without prejudice to the status of or sovereignty over any territory, to the delimitation of international frontiers and boundaries and to the name of any territory, city or area.

The statistical data for Israel are supplied by and under the responsibility of the relevant Israeli authorities. The use of such data by the OECD is without prejudice to the status of the Golan Heights, East Jerusalem and Israeli settlements in the West Bank under the terms of international law.

Note by the Republic of Türkiye
The information in this document with reference to "Cyprus" relates to the southern part of the Island. There is no single authority representing both Turkish and Greek Cypriot people on the Island. Türkiye recognises the Turkish Republic of Northern Cyprus (TRNC). Until a lasting and equitable solution is found within the context of the United Nations, Türkiye shall preserve its position concerning the "Cyprus issue".

Note by all the European Union Member States of the OECD and the European Union
The Republic of Cyprus is recognised by all members of the United Nations with the exception of Türkiye. The information in this document relates to the area under the effective control of the Government of the Republic of Cyprus.

Please cite this publication as:
OECD (2024), *Pricing Greenhouse Gas Emissions 2024: Gearing Up to Bring Emissions Down*, OECD Series on Carbon Pricing and Energy Taxation, OECD Publishing, Paris, https://doi.org/10.1787/b44c74e6-en.

ISBN 978-92-64-33723-7 (print)
ISBN 978-92-64-75053-1 (PDF)
ISBN 978-92-64-57712-1 (HTML)
ISBN 978-92-64-18035-2 (epub)

OECD Series on Carbon Pricing and Energy Taxation
ISSN 2958-0161 (print)
ISSN 2957-9899 (online)

Photo credits: Cover © Bene_A/Shutterstock.com.

Corrigenda to OECD publications may be found at: https://www.oecd.org/en/publications/support/corrigenda.html.

Foreword

This report was prepared by the Tax Policy and Statistics division of the OECD's Centre for Tax Policy and Administration. It is published as part of the OECD series on Carbon Pricing and Energy Taxation (CPET), which earlier included the first iteration of this report, *Pricing Greenhouse Gas Emissions: Turning Climate Targets into Climate Action*, and *Effective Carbon Rates 2023*, which focused on emissions trading systems (ETSs) and included an in-depth analysis of the relevant free allocation and price stability mechanisms. This report, *Pricing Greenhouse Gas Emissions 2024: Gearing Up to Bring Emissions Down,* now covers 79 countries, reflecting broader coverage, and tracks the evolution of carbon and energy pricing instruments between 2021 and 2023.

The report and underlying database provide a comprehensive stocktake of effective carbon and energy rates. Specifically, they track and describe trends in carbon taxes, emissions trading systems (ETSs), fuel excise taxes and their associated emission bases, and the resulting indicator: Effective Carbon Rates (ECRs). They also track and describe electricity excise taxes and the abovementioned policies and their associated energy bases in the Effective Energy Rates (EERs) indicator. In addition, the report captures negative rates through fossil fuel and electricity subsidies that can reduce the price signal of carbon and energy pricing illustrated, resulting in the additional indicators of the Net Effective Carbon Rate (Net ECRs) and Net Effective Energy Rates (Net EERs) that altogether form the basis for the *Carbon Pricing and Energy Taxation* (CPET) database. The report uses the CPET database to analyse the latest trends and developments in carbon pricing and energy taxation policy.

The project was led by Jacob Smith under the guidance of Assia Elgouacem and the overall responsibility of Kurt Van Dender. The report was drafted by Jacob Smith, Insa Handschuch and Lotta Hambrecht with critical inputs from Konstantinos Theodoropoulos, Mark Mateo and Stéphane Buydens.

The CPET database design and maintenance are coordinated by Konstantinos Theodoropoulos. Database updates were conducted by Konstantinos Theodoropoulos, Astrid Tricaud, Insa Handschuch, Nathan Ducrocq, Lotta Hambrecht, Jacob Smith and Tina Aubrun. Information on ETSs from 2022 were from the Effective Carbon Rates 2023 database, updated by Anasuya Raj and Konstantinos Theodoropoulos.

The integration of selected fossil fuel support measures from the OECD Inventory of Support Measures for Fossil Fuels into the Taxing Energy Use and Effective Carbon Rates database is the result of a collaboration with Dylan Bourny and the Data and Modelling Division in the OECD's Trade and Agriculture Directorate.

The authors would like the thank the large team of OECD colleagues that assisted with feedback and data collection at different stages of the production of the report, including but not limited to Anasuya Raj and Jonas Teusch.

The OECD is grateful to the Kingdom of Belgium Federal Public Service, Foreign Affairs, Foreign Trade and Development Cooperation for a voluntary contribution that has supported this work.

Table of contents

FIGURES

TABLES

BOXES

Executive summary

To progress the transition to net-zero emissions, countries must ramp up action to meet climate goals. Achieving the 2030 Nationally Determined Contributions (NDCs) targets, as well as peak fossil fuel use and GHG emissions, requires narrowing the implementation gap in current climate policies. In this context, although progress in carbon pricing and transforming energy taxation slowed down or even regressed amidst the global energy crisis, a number of jurisdictions are now preparing for progressing carbon pricing with a view to achieving their climate goals.

Pricing Greenhouse Gas Emissions 2024: Gearing Up to Bring Emissions Down tracks how explicit carbon pricing instruments as well as specific taxes and subsidies on energy use have evolved between 2021 and 2023 across 79 countries, covering approximately 82% of global greenhouse gas (GHG) emissions. This report focuses on emissions trading systems (ETSs), carbon taxes, fuel and electricity excise taxes, as well as subsidies that lower pre-tax prices on emissions or energy products. The tax rates for this edition reflect rates applicable on 1 April 2023 while emissions trading systems implemented throughout 2023 are also included. While these instruments represent an important subset of instruments with important implications for emissions outcomes, governments take diverse approaches to meet their climate targets.

At first glance, momentum in carbon pricing and energy taxation appears to have stalled since 2021. Although some countries have introduced new carbon pricing instruments, and some have been expanded, or tightened emissions caps, overall progress on expanding emission coverage has slowed. This is due to a large share of emissions already covered by major economies, as well as lasting effects from the response to the shock of the global energy crisis in 2022. The energy crisis caused countries to increase support measures, including through rate reductions or exemptions of energy taxes, subsidies and delaying or cancelling planned advancements in carbon and energy pricing. While these reductions in overall carbon rates dominate results, a closer look shows that these are concentrated in implicit carbon pricing such as fuel excise taxes, whereas explicit carbon pricing through ETSs and carbon taxes have made modest increases. Meanwhile, economies are introducing new, and expanding existing, carbon pricing instruments. Increasingly, they are paying attention to international effects of asymmetries across borders and are introducing or considering introducing instruments such as Border Carbon Adjustments and investment subsidies for low-emission technologies as part of plans to meet fast-approaching climate targets in 2030. Additionally, progress is being made through expansion to include additional industries in carbon pricing schemes. Finally, governments are considering the public acceptability of mitigation policies like carbon pricing, including through revenue use and tax base shifting strategies.

The report also finds that:

Overall, the share of emissions covered by an explicit carbon price and fuel excise taxes in 2023 has remained unchanged compared with the share of emissions covered in 2021. Approximately 42% of GHG emissions across the 79 countries covered in this report are subject to a positive *Net Effective Carbon Rate* (Net ECR), accounting for carbon taxes, emissions trading systems, fuel excise taxes and fossil fuel subsidies. About 27% of GHG emissions in 2023 are covered by explicit carbon prices – an ETS, a carbon tax, or both - while the share covered by fuel excise taxes, an implicit form of carbon pricing, is lower at 23%.

The change in rates has been mixed. Overall, the average Net ECR declined to EUR 14.0/tCO_2e in 2023 from EUR 17.9/tCO_2e in 2021. Explicit carbon prices increased, primarily reflecting the increase in average ETS permit price and modest carbon tax increases. Implicit carbon prices in the form of fuel excise taxes remain the strongest price signal, despite decreasing relative to 2021 levels. This was accompanied by an increase in fossil fuel subsidies.

To a large extent, the downward shift in Net ECRs reflect countries' responses to the shock of the energy crisis of 2022. In an effort to address concerns over energy affordability and security, governments ramped up fossil fuel subsidies and introduced rate reductions and exemptions to fuel excise taxes. As a result, the Net ECR of road transport, buildings and agriculture strongly declined between 2021 and 2023. Road transport remains priced at the highest average Net ECR across sectors, despite a substantial decrease of 24%.

Currently, an increase in the introduction of new carbon pricing instruments is expected over the next five years. In particular, ETSs are likely to become more widely used and diverse, with new systems under development that could lead to an increase in coverage of global emissions of 7 percentage points, i.e. an increase by about one quarter. Expansions of existing carbon pricing instruments to more complex sectors such as waste incineration have also moved into focus.

Assessing the taxation of fuel and electricity use through the *Effective Energy Rate* (EER) shows that more than half of energy use remains untaxed in 2023. Measured in EUR/GJ, the EER applies to energy use as a base, accounting for fuel and electricity excise taxes and explicit carbon pricing instruments. On average, high-income countries taxed energy use at EUR 4.96/GJ in 2023, while low-upper and middle-income economies levied on average EUR 0.54/GJ. In both groups, the EER's distribution remains heavily skewed due to differentiated rates across sectors, fuels and consumer groups within a country and differences of tax levels between countries.

Fuel excise taxes continue to dominate EER in 2023, contributing on average 74% to a country's EER. However, for the first time, four countries increased their level of explicit carbon pricing to the extent that they levy a higher explicit carbon price than fuel excise taxes per GJ.

Fossil fuel use is subject to a higher Net EER than low-carbon electricity sources. The road transport fuels, gasoline and diesel, continue to face the highest rate. A notable change since 2021 was the Net EER of coal becoming higher than natural gas in 2023 due to higher subsidies for the latter. All low-carbon electricity sources are subject to the lowest Net EERs, with solar, wind and nuclear power effectively being subsidised.

Hikes in fuel and electricity prices during the energy crisis in 2022 triggered many governments to adopt large fiscal support packages, including both significant cuts to fuel excise taxes and increases in subsidies for fossil fuels and electricity. Similar to the Net ECR, this has driven the Net EER downwards since 2021 in many countries. While many countries have phased out temporary measures, some have chosen to maintain support.

Untargeted price-suppressing policies such as cuts to fuel excise tax or VAT rates and caps on energy retail prices dominated government responses to the energy crisis. Broad-based measures effectively subsidised the energy consumption of all households, not providing important incentives to reduce energy demand.

Global revenue losses from displaced oil consumption due to rapidly electrifying road transport sector stood at EUR 13.2 billion in 2023 and could in increase to more than EUR 155 billion in 2035. Governments started adjusting policy frameworks, with recent examples resulting in a shift away from energy taxes towards other pricing mechanisms such as distance-based road user charges.

At the time of writing this report, 42% of emissions are covered by a positive Net ECR and 27% by an explicit carbon price, though the pricing level remains at a Net ECR of EUR 14.0/tCO_2e. This will require an increase from between EUR 60/tCO_2e and EUR 120/tCO_2e by 2030 to meet climate goals, or the use of other policies that may induce similar emission reductions as these carbon price levels.

While the overall emissions coverage has changed little, underlying changes such as the introduction of new ETSs in middle-income countries, the expansion of existing instruments to cover new sectors such as waste incineration, the introduction of instruments to cover carbon content in imports and supporting policies for investment in low-emission assets are resulting in a web of complementary policies to achieve countries' political, economic, social and environmental goals.

In addition, the effects of the energy crisis have negatively impacted the Net ECR via reductions in fuel excise tax rates and increases in fossil fuel subsidies. While these changes were not the direct result of a change in carbon pricing policy – explicit carbon rates through carbon taxes and ETSs have seen moderate increases in rates since the last edition – they weaken incentives to reduce emissions.

It has become clear in recent years that there is no silver bullet for carbon pricing and energy policy as countries have opted for a complex array of policy instruments to mitigate climate change that suit their economic, political and social circumstances. As policy action ramps up, the challenge increasingly is to understand policy interactions internationally. In relation to climate policy effectiveness, governments are exploring options to reduce carbon leakage concerns e.g. in the form of free allocation of emission permits and Border Carbon Adjustments.

1 Introduction and methodology

This chapter outlines the current state of carbon pricing and energy taxation and describes the methodology underpinning the *Pricing Greenhouse Gas Emissions* series. It provides an overview of the *Carbon Pricing and Energy Taxation* database including the coverage of instruments, countries and sectors. The chapter then details the methodology for computing the key indicators – Net Effective Carbon Rate and Net Effective Energy Rate – that are used to measure changes in global carbon pricing and energy taxation. The analysis covers carbon taxes, emissions trading systems, fuel excise taxes, electricity taxes and subsidies that lower pre-tax energy prices for 79 economies in this edition, representing 82% of global emissions. Last, the chapter outlines the methodologies for additional analyses presented in the subsequent chapters.

1.1. The time for deep emissions reductions is fast approaching

It is widely acknowledged that addressing the risks of climate change demands significant economic and structural transformations and these can be incentivised by the implementation of carbon pricing and other climate policies to steer economies towards a net-zero future. The IPCC, in their latest findings and with a high level of confidence, report that greenhouse gas (GHG) emissions have unequivocally caused global warming through unsustainable energy use, lifestyles and patterns of consumption and production (IPCC, 2023[1]). In response, the Paris Agreement offers countries the flexibility to chart their paths toward these ambitious goals and as a result, the global economy could be on track to reach peak emissions before 2030 (IEA, 2023[2]). In order to further reduce emissions while at the same time managing growth in total energy supply, governments must close the gap between existing policies and those under development (the 'implementation gap'), as well as the gap between the current and necessary level of ambition required to meet global climate goals (the 'ambition gap') (Figure 1.1). As outlined in this report, in order to achieve climate goals, the need for a deep reductions in emissions – a period of rapid and drastic reductions in the generation of emissions through climate policies - is imminent (IPCC, 2023[1]).

Figure 1.1. Achieving net-zero requires deep reductions before 2030

Emissions and energy consumption pathways for net zero by 2050

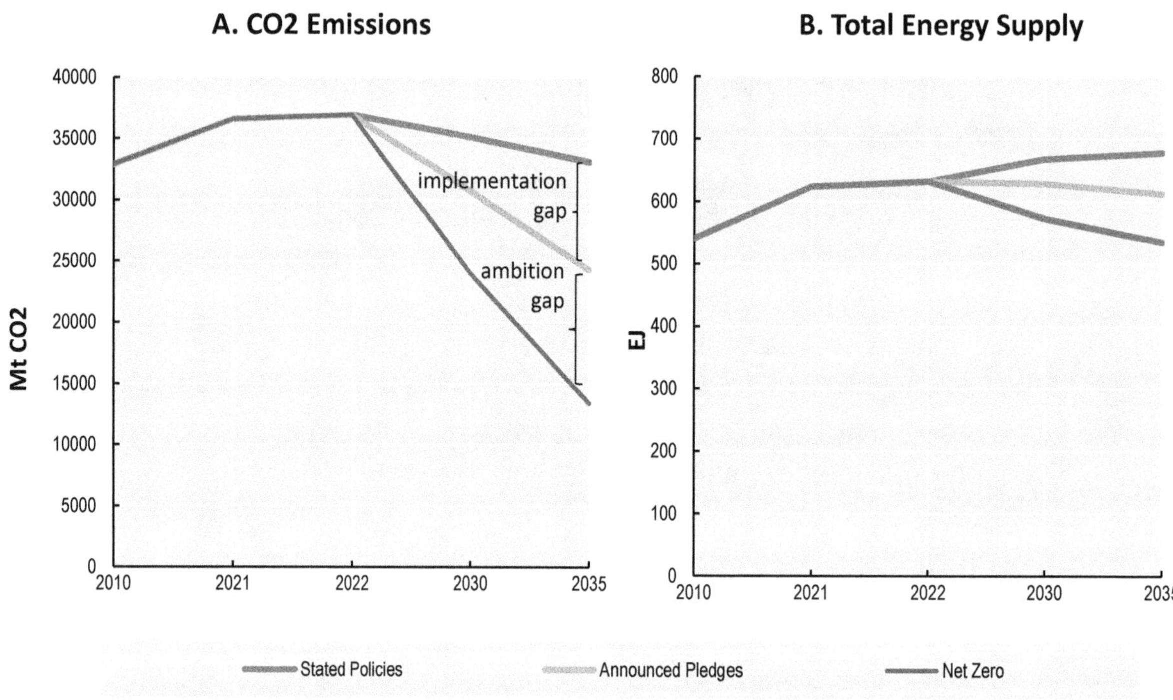

Note: The IEA models three scenarios for the global energy sector. The Stated Policies Scenario (STEPS) gives a sense of the energy system progression, based on a detailed review of the current policy landscape and provides a conservative benchmark for the future by not taking for granted that governments will achieve all announced climate ambitions. The Announced Pledges Scenario (APS) illustrates the extent to which announced ambitions and targets can deliver the emissions reductions needed to achieve net zero emissions by 2050. The Net Zero Emissions by 2050 Scenario (NZE Scenario) is a normative scenario that shows a pathway for the global energy sector to achieve net zero CO_2 emissions by 2050. (IEA, 2023[3]).
Source: (IEA, 2023[4]).

While Effective Carbon Rates have been increasing over recent years, in many countries rates remain low relative to the level needed to achieve upcoming climate targets (OECD, 2022[5]; Stiglitz et al., 2017[6]). Emissions trading systems (ETS) in particular are gaining traction, but still a large number remain in their pilot or transitory phases and offer high levels of free allocations that reduce incentives to invest in cleaner technologies (OECD, 2023[7]). Carbon pricing instruments can drive behavioural changes across industries and households, aligning economic activities with the urgent need to mitigate climate change impacts. The shift from preparation to action is critical as the window for preventing the most catastrophic outcomes of climate change narrows, requiring increasingly decisive action (IPCC, 2023[1]).

This report provides an in-depth analysis of the current global trends in carbon pricing and energy taxation based on 79 covered countries, shedding light on both the progress that characterise today's carbon pricing and energy taxation landscape, as well as examining some pathways forward. By measuring the price and coverage of various carbon pricing and energy taxation instruments, the report aims to provide a clear picture of how these tools are being utilised. It highlights the uneven implementation of carbon pricing and energy taxation and the diversity in system design across different regions and sectors, underscoring the complex dynamics that may influence the effectiveness and efficiency of these measures in reducing emissions.

The report begins with an overview of the context that surrounds carbon pricing and energy taxation, followed by an explanation of the indicators and methodology of the analysis (Chapter 1). It then explores the trends in carbon pricing and coverage since 2021, an estimation of upcoming emissions coverage, and delves into the practical consideration for the implementation of carbon pricing and the role of revenues use in public and political feasibility (Chapter 2). Next, the report outlines trends in energy taxation, including coverage and price trends, and then explores how energy taxation can be better aligned with climate policy and other goals. This includes the role of energy affordability and security as well as transitioning tax bases as the energy mix shifts from combustibles to renewables (Chapter 3).

1.2. Methodology: A systematic stocktaking of carbon pricing and energy taxation

1.2.1. Overview of the report series, databases and covered policy instruments

The *Pricing Greenhouse Gas Emissions report* – first published in 2022 – is an evolution from the *Taxing Energy Use report* and includes data and findings from the *Effective Carbon Rates* report which together make up the *OECD Series on Carbon Pricing and Energy Taxation*. The respective databases of the two series have been merged to form the *Carbon Pricing and Energy Taxation* database (CPET) (Figure 1.2). Although the *Pricing Greenhouse Gas Emissions* series draws on the most up-to-date data from the *Effective Carbon Rates* series, the data collection exercises and focus of the reports differ. The *Effective Carbon Rates* series comments on changes related to the Effective Carbon Rates indicator, mainly focussing on those resulting from developments in ETSs, including the interaction between free allocations and Effective Carbon Rates (OECD, 2023[7]). The *Pricing Greenhouse Gas Emissions* series is broader and collects data on carbon taxes, fuel excise taxes, energy taxes and complements this with the OECD's *Effective Carbon Rates* database on ETSs, the OECD's *Inventory of Fossil Fuel Support* database on fossil fuel subsidies and other emissions and energy use data from the IEA. Due to a time lag in fossil fuel subsidy data (2022 data in this case), this edition notes that the ongoing changes in subsidy measures sometimes may not reflect the most up-to-date policy measures. These main data sources are used to produce two distinct indicators, the Net Effective Carbon Rate (Net ECR) and Net Effective Energy Rate (Net EER). They are the basis to produce a comprehensive analysis of the latest development in carbon pricing and energy taxation policies across the world.

Figure 1.2. The evolution and elements of the Pricing Greenhouse Gas Emissions report

A timeline of the OECD's Taxing Energy Use, Effective Carbon Rates, and Pricing Greenhouse Gas Emissions reports

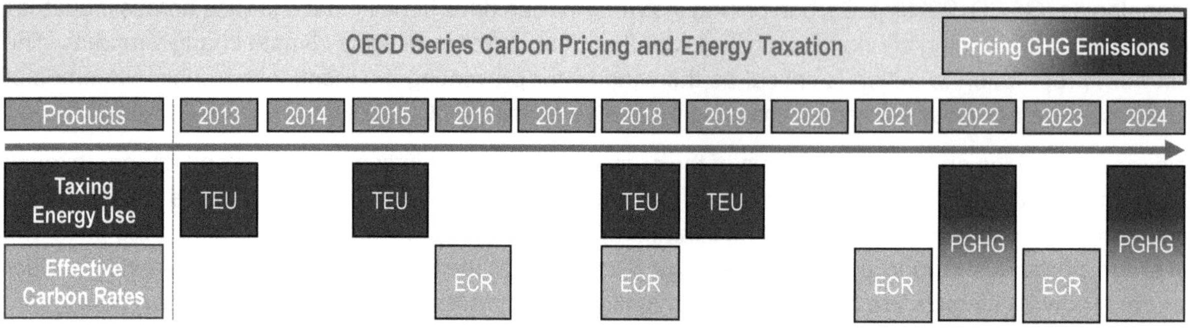

Source: Authors.

1.2.2. Coverage update

The CPET database focuses on pricing instruments that apply to a base that is proportional to an energy or GHG emissions base (Table 1.1). It therefore excludes taxes and fees that are only partially correlated with energy use or GHG emissions. Common examples of policy instruments that fall outside the scope of the database include vehicle purchase taxes, registration or circulation taxes, and taxes that are directly levied on non-GHG emissions. Some countries also apply production taxes on the extraction or exploitation of energy resources (e.g., severance taxes on oil extraction). Since these supply-side measures are not directly linked to domestic energy use or emissions, the database does not cover them.

Similarly, the database does not include value added taxes (VAT) or sales taxes as in principle these rates apply equally to a wide range of goods and therefore do not change the relative prices of products or services. In practice there are some exceptions to these whereby preferential rates are applied to products such that they change the relative price of carbon- or energy-intensive products, compared to less carbon- or energy-intensive products. Although this does not warrant including VAT explicitly in the database, it is explored briefly in this report to demonstrate how VAT rates can play a role in carbon pricing in some specific cases.

In addition, explicit carbon pricing and energy taxation are not the only instruments necessary or available to achieve net-zero. Many countries are opting for a complex mix of policies that do not directly price emission or energy bases, such as subsidies for low-emission investment. These policies can also influence the relative prices of emissions and energy products through other channels and, in turn, the behaviour of households and firms. Such policies must be acknowledged as part of the climate policies package, along with carbon pricing and energy taxation, that will lead to the climate goals with different considerations and means for different countries.

Table 1.1. Policy instruments covered and databases used in this report

Policy Instrument	Definition	Examples	Composite indicator	Dataset
ETS	The price of tradable emission permits in mandatory emissions trading and cap-and-trade systems representing the opportunity cost of emitting an extra unit of CO_2e., regardless of the permit allocation method	Emissions trading systems are most commonly used for larger emitters from the power and industry sectors and are in operation in, e.g., California (United States) and Québec (Canada), China, and the European Union	Component of Effective Carbon Rate (ECR) and Net ECR (Chapter 2) as well as Effective Energy Rate (EER) and Net EER (Chapter 3)	Included in both GHG emissions dataset (expressed per tCO_2e, (Chapter 2) and energy content dataset (expressed per GJ, Chapter 3)
Carbon tax	All taxes for which the rate is explicitly linked to the carbon content of the fuel or where the tax is levied directly on GHG emissions (irrespective of whether the resulting carbon price is uniform across fuels and GHGs.) The term carbon tax is thus equally used for taxes that apply to GHGs other than CO_2	Most countries administer explicit carbon taxes in the same way as fuel excise taxes (e.g. France, Sweden). Countries that follow this fuel-based approach do not actually tax CO_2 directly, but rather calculate the corresponding rate in common commercial units, for instance by reference to kilograms for solid fuels, liters for liquid fuels, and cubic meters for gaseous fuels. Fuel-based carbon taxes are often levied as a component of fuel excise taxes. There are a number of countries that tax GHGs directly. Countries that pursue such an emissions-based approach include Chile, Estonia, Latvia and South Africa.	Component of ECR, Net ECR, EER, and Net EER	Included in both GHG emissions dataset (expressed per tCO_2e) and energy content dataset (expressed per GJ)
Fuel excise tax	All excise taxes that are levied on fuels and that are not carbon taxes	Almost all countries tax gasoline and diesel used for road transport. The tax rate is typically specified per litre or gallon of fuel.	Component of ECR, Net ECR, EER, and Net EER	Included in both GHG emissions dataset (expressed per tCO_2e) and energy content dataset (expressed per GJ)
Fossil fuel subsidy	Budgetary transfers that decrease pre-tax prices for domestic fossil fuel use.	There are countries that regulate the price of fossil fuels below supply costs and then compensate fuel suppliers for the resulting losses (e.g. LPG in Morocco).	Component of Net ECR and Net EER	Included in both GHG emissions dataset (expressed per tCO_2e) and energy content dataset (expressed per GJ)
Electricity excise tax	All excise taxes that are levied on electricity.	Mandatory for residential and commercial electricity use in the European Union. Often specified per kWh of electricity end use.	Component of EER and Net EER	Only included in energy content dataset (expressed per GJ)
Electricity subsidy	Budgetary transfers that decrease pre-tax prices for domestic electricity use.	In some countries, such as Nigeria, the government provides budgetary transfers to electricity suppliers to finance the shortfall resulting from electricity tariffs that are set below supply costs.	Component of Net EER	Only included in energy content dataset (expressed per GJ)

Note: Data on the tax policy instruments are collected via publicly available official sources; government officials are provided with the opportunity to review and refine the data. Excises are taxes levied as a product specific tax on a predefined limited range of goods (OECD, 2023[8]). For details on emissions trading systems, see the OECD's (2023[7]) Effective Carbon Rates 2023. For details on fossil fuel and electricity subsidies, see (OECD, 2023[9]; Garsous et al., 2023[10]).
Source: (OECD, 2022[5]).

This edition of the CPET database covers 79 countries, an increase in geographic coverage from 71 in 2022, and from 44 in 2019. The database coverage has been expanded to additional countries including Croatia, Bulgaria, Romania, Kazakhstan, Malta, Mauritius, Singapore and Zambia. This edition includes all OECD and G20 countries except Saudi Arabia, and for the first time, also covers all European Union (EU) member states. As a result, the database covers approximately 82% of global GHG emissions (excluding emissions from land use change and forestry). Where time trends with regard to previous editions are presented (concerning data for 2018 and 2021), the coverage and country composition of the database differs year-by-year, which sometimes does not allow for direct comparisons.

As in previous editions, the database covers six economic sectors that account for CO_2 emissions from energy use in road transport, off-road transport, industry, agriculture and fisheries, buildings, electricity (Table 1.2). GHG emissions and energy use are assigned to the sector in which the primary energy is consumed. A seventh sector captures other GHG emissions, which are separated due to data limitations and to facilitate comparisons with previous vintages. Table A.1 in the Annex contains further details on how energy products are aggregated in the database. In line with previous editions, this report presents results that exclude emissions from the combustion of biofuels, consistent with the practice that the other GHG emissions (emissions from CH_4, N_2O, F-gases and process CO_2 emissions) that were added to the emissions base exclude LUCF.

Table 1.2. Definitions of CPET sectors

Sector	Base definition in GHG emissions dataset (Chapter 2)	Base definition in energy content dataset (Chapter 3)
Road	Fossil fuel CO_2 emissions from all primary energy used in road transport	Energy content (in joules) of all primary energy used in road transport.
Off-road	Fossil fuel CO_2 emissions from all primary energy used in off-road transport (incl. pipelines, rail transport, aviation and maritime transport). Fuels used in international aviation and maritime transport are not included.	Energy content (in joules) of all primary energy used in off-road transport (incl. pipelines, rail transport, aviation and maritime transport). Fuels used in international aviation and maritime transport are not included
Industry	Fossil fuel CO_2 emissions from primary energy used in industrial facilities (incl. district heating and auto-producer electricity plants).	Energy content (in joules) of all primary energy used in off-road transport (incl. pipelines, rail transport, aviation and maritime transport). Fuels used in international aviation and maritime transport are not included.
Agriculture & Fisheries	Fossil fuel CO_2 emissions from primary energy used in agriculture, fisheries and forestry for activities other than electricity generation and transport	Energy content (in joules) of all primary energy used in industrial facilities (incl. district heating and auto-producer electricity plants).
Buildings	Fossil fuel CO_2 emissions from primary energy used by households, commercial and public services for activities other than electricity generation and transport.	Energy content (in joules) of all primary energy used by households, commercial and public services for activities other than electricity generation and transport
Electricity	Fossil fuel CO_2 emissions from primary energy used to generate electricity (excl. auto-producer electricity plants which are assigned to industry), including for electricity exports. Electricity imports are excluded.	Energy content (in joules) of all primary energy used to generate electricity (excl. auto-producer electricity plants which are assigned to industry), including for electricity exports. Electricity imports are only used for the calculation of net energy tax revenues (as imported electricity is typically also subject to electricity excise taxes where they exist).
Other GHG (excl. LUCF)	All other GHG emissions include methane, nitrous oxide from agriculture, fugitive emissions from oil, gas and coal mining activities, waste and industrial processes, as well as non-fuel combustion CO_2 emissions from industrial processes (mainly cement production) and F-gas emissions. Excludes LUCF emissions. Excludes CO_2 emissions from fuel combustion which are reported in the agriculture & fisheries sector.	Not applicable.

Note: Estimates of primary energy use are based on the territoriality principle, and include energy sold in the territory of a country but potentially used elsewhere (e.g. because of fuel tourism in road transport).
Source: Own classification based on information on energy flows contained in the IEA's (2023[11]) extended world energy balances and "other GHG" reported in Climate Watch's (2024[12]) GHG emissions dataset.

Indicators of Pricing Greenhouse Gas Emissions and their components

Pricing Greenhouse Gas Emissions features two main indicators – the Net Effective Carbon Rate (Net ECR), representing the effective tax rate on GHG emissions (measured in EUR/tCO_2e), and the Net Effective Energy Rate (Net EER), representing the effective tax rate on energy use (measured in EUR/GJ), both net of subsidies. Although these indicators are related through the overlap in policy instruments included, the rates collected under these indicators apply to different bases – emissions versus energy. These different bases do not cover the same economic activities and therefore cannot be directly compared or converted into each other, even though energy use and emissions are correlated. As a result, the Net ECR and Net EER indicators cannot be compared to each other (Figure 1.3). For this reason, this report discusses the indicators separately, with Chapter 2 focussing on the Net ECRs and related developments in carbon pricing policies, while Chapter 3 focussing on Net EERs and related trends in energy taxation.

Both indicators are a representation of *effective* rates, meaning tax exemptions, rate reductions and refunds and other preferential tax treatment are accounted for in the final estimate. These measures are common in carbon pricing and energy taxation systems, as certain emitters or energy users often receive preferential treatment that reduces the effective tax paid on emissions or energy use.

The *net* effective rates take into account negative carbon pricing or energy policy instruments resulting from consumption subsidies that lower pre-tax energy prices below reference prices. Changes in subsidies result from not only from policy changes, such as changes in the regulated pre-tax price, but also from changes in the reference price and therefore fluctuate with market conditions (e.g. an increase in the reference price, all else equal, would result in an increase in the subsidy amount and thus a higher negative price). This is unlike instruments such as carbon taxes and fuel excise taxes, which are not normally driven by broader market forces, but more by policy intervention. Together with preferential treatment, subsidies lower the price paid on emissions and energy.

The Effective Carbon Rate (ECR) and the Net Effective Carbon Rate (Net ECR)

The ECR is the sum of carbon taxes, ETS permit prices and fuel excise taxes, representing the aggregate Effective Carbon Rate paid on emissions. To combine the *marginal* price signals of the various instruments, fuel excise tax and fuel-based carbon tax rates (which are typically expressed in physical units such as litres or kilogrammes) are converted into tax rates per tonne of CO_2-equivalent based on the carbon content of the fuels that they apply to. Other emission-based carbon taxes, as well as ETS permit prices do not need to be converted, as they are typically expressed in tonne of CO_2-equivalent.

The ECR indicator in this report is primarily the Effective *Marginal* Carbon Rate (EMCR, referred to as ECR in this report unless otherwise noted), which is distinct from the Effective *Average* Carbon Rate (EACR). The difference between these two measures is that the EACR accounts for free allocation of permits in ETSs by including emissions that are covered with free allocations as part of the total emissions base. This reduces the average permit price across the emissions base, compared to EMCR. This is further outlined in detail in the Effective Carbon Rates 2023 report (OECD, 2023[7]).

The *Net* ECR is a different indicator that attempts to account for negative carbon prices in the form of fossil fuel subsidies that decrease pre-tax prices of domestic fossil fuel use and may counteract the price signals from fuel excise taxes, carbon taxes and ETS permit prices. These subsidies are collected through the CPET database, drawing on direct budgetary transfer data of the OECD *Inventory of Fossil Fuel Support Measures* database for OECD and G20 countries, and other desk research. They are mapped onto the CO_2 emissions from domestic energy use that are directly affected by the measures and are then converted into a negative tax rate per tonne of CO_2. This process excludes tax expenditures on taxes that are already recorded as the effective rates through tax reductions, exemptions and refunds in the CPET database, but adds budgetary transfers to fuel suppliers, electricity suppliers and end users (Garsous et al., 2023[10]).

This creates a distinct indicator from the ECR, where the Net ECR includes policy instruments applying to a base not strictly proportional to emissions, and estimates the negative prices resulting from subsidies and how these evolve over time across countries, fuels and sectors.

The Effective Energy Rate (EER) and Net Effective Energy Rate (Net EER)

The EER is composed of carbon taxes, ETS permit prices, fuel excise taxes and electricity excise taxes that are applied to an energy base that results in an effective rate. The rates are converted into tax rates per gigajoule of energy, based on the energy content of the energy product of which they apply. Like the previous ECR indicator, the rates used in this report, unless otherwise stated, are marginal effective rates and therefore do not account for free allocation.

The *Net* EER is a distinct indicator that attempts to estimate and account for fossil fuel subsidies and electricity subsidies as negative energy rates. In general, electricity excise taxes and subsidies tend to not treat fossil fuels in a differential manner compared to lower-emitting energy sources and are typically also applied to energy sources that do not emit CO_2 emissions such as hydro, solar, as well as nuclear (OECD, 2019[13]; OECD, 2022[5]). Altogether, the Net EER captures the interaction of both positive and negative price signals on energy use, including electricity, but does not include the comprehensive range of levies that apply to electricity.

Figure 1.3. Net Effective Carbon and Net Effective Energy Rates: how they relate

The components and the different bases used

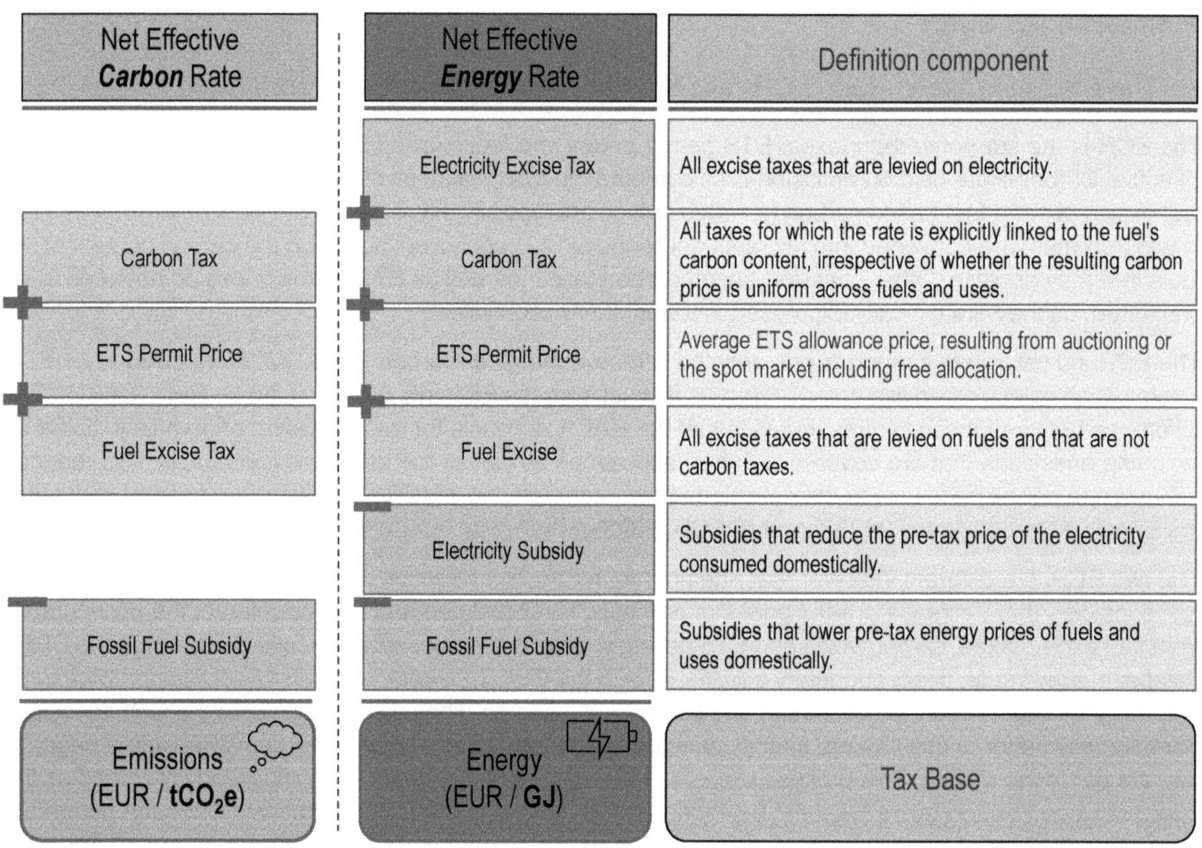

Source: Authors.

1.2.3. Mapping tax rates to their respective GHG emission and energy bases

The first step of the methodology is collecting data on carbon pricing and energy taxation rates, as detailed above. The second step is to map tax rates and subsidies to their respective emissions and energy bases, in order to compute both the ECR and EER, and then the Net ECR and Net EER. This is done through assigning tax rates to the latest available information on energy use, by energy product, adapted from the IEA's *World Energy Statistics and Balances* (2023[11]). This is also used to calculate CO_2 emissions from energy use, together with non-CO_2 GHG emissions from energy use sourced from Climate Watch (2024[12]). To produce the final indicators, for the Net ECR, all positive components including rates from carbon taxes, ETS and fuel excise taxes, are summed with the negative pricing components resulting from fossil fuel subsidies. For the Net EER, the positive components also include electricity taxes and the negative components also include electricity subsidies. After mapping of net tax rates to the emissions/energy bases, the weighted rates can be aggregated to create net effective rates by country, instrument, and sectors. All rates are therefore in EUR/tCO_2e for the Net ECR or EUR/GJ for the Net EER based on the carbon content and energy content of the product, respectively. Official OECD exchange rates and inflation data are used to express all prices in real 2023 euros.

The mapping accounts for overlaps between policy instruments, which is common across countries and instruments. In some cases, policies are implemented to take effect together (e.g. a carbon tax applied to emissions that are also covered by an ETS, as in the case of the United Kingdom), whereas in other cases, policies are implemented to cover specific sectors or uses (e.g. a carbon tax applied only to emissions that are not already covered by an ETS, as in the case of France). Ignoring such interactions, which vary across countries and levels of governance (supranational, national, subnational), would be an inaccurate representation of the coverage and prices of countries' carbon pricing and energy taxation policies.

In most countries, carbon pricing and energy taxation is applied at the national level. However, there are some exceptions, such as the United States, Canada, Mexico and China, where subnational instruments play a significant role and are included. To assign subnational rates to their corresponding emissions or energy use bases, it is necessary to split countries' emissions and energy bases by subnational jurisdictions, as the IEA's World Energy Statistics and Balances report energy use data at the country level.[1] Where possible, CPET relies on energy use data from official sources, however simplifying assumptions are required to account for some of these instruments.

1.3. Methodologies for in-depth analysis

In addition to the main indicators, this edition of *Pricing Greenhouse Gas Emissions* presents several counterfactual exercises, bringing together data from the CPET database with other policy developments in carbon pricing and energy taxation (Table 1.3). These exercises include an estimate of changes to the coverage of Effective Carbon Rates resulting from policies that are currently under development; revenue potential from comprehensive carbon pricing reform (including phasing out free allocation, fossil fuel subsidies, and setting a minimum Effective Carbon Rate); and effects on revenue through a shift in the tax base from combustibles to electricity in the road transport sector. These counterfactual scenarios provide an in-depth exploration of a selection of possible developments across carbon pricing and energy taxation and demonstrate the potential for further analysis that can be conducted using this database.

Table 1.3. Counterfactual scenarios

Outline of additional quantitative analyses undertaken

Counterfactual	Indicator	Goal	Chapter
Implementation of carbon pricing instruments currently under development	Effective Marginal Carbon Rates – Coverage	Estimate an upper bound of the changes in coverage of emissions that may occur from the implementation of explicit carbon pricing policies that are currently under development (and may be implemented in coming years) across countries, illustrating the in-progress efforts across countries.	2
Carbon pricing policy reform	Net Effective Average Carbon Rates – Revenue potential	Demonstrate the additional revenue that could be raised from a comprehensive reform of carbon pricing policy, that includes the phasing out free allocations, phasing out fossil fuel subsidies and setting a minimum Effective Carbon Rate of EUR 60-120/tCO_2e.	2
Tax base shifting	Effective Average Energy Rates - Revenue	Inform about changes in tax bases and estimated revenue impacts through a shift of energy consumption from combustibles to electricity, with a focus on the road transport sector.	3

1.3.1. Emissions coverage from carbon pricing instrument under development

With countries progressing carbon pricing at different rates, there are a large number of instruments, mostly ETSs, that have not been implemented but are still under development and likely to take effect in the coming years. To illustrate the ongoing efforts in carbon pricing policies, this edition of *Pricing Greenhouse Gas Emissions* estimates the change in the share of emissions subject to a positive price that could result from these instruments being implemented.

A stocktake of instruments that are under development are drawn from the World Bank's State and Trends of Carbon Pricing Dashboard, whereby instruments are categorised as such if the country's government is actively working towards the implementation of the instrument, a mandate may have been established, but regulated entities do not yet face compliance obligations, and this has been formally confirmed by government sources (The World Bank, 2024[14]). Instruments at the regional, national and subnational level for countries covered by the CPET database, are considered. Available details on the planned coverage of these instruments, primarily in terms of fuels and sectors, are matched to the IEA's (2023[11]) World Energy Balances and Statistics and Climate Watch (2024[12]) data as is done in the general methodology of *Pricing Greenhouse Gas Emissions*. While some countries have more granular information on the planned emissions threshold determining which entities are covered by the instrument, these are not accounted for in this exercise due to data constraints. Where there is a lack of information on planned implementation, additional assumptions are made to be able to model the instrument. Overlaps between the emissions coverage of new instruments and existing explicit carbon pricing instruments are accounted for. All policies are assumed to be implemented under the current environment, although the timeline of implementation is not finalised for most of the instruments covered.

Given the variability in available information and assumptions made, the estimates should be interpreted as an upper bound of the expected change in emissions coverage as some instruments under development may not be implemented or the actual implementation may result in smaller changes than estimated in this exercise due to the assumptions made. However, it is possible that additional new schemes are also implemented. Nevertheless, the analysis can provide an indicative quantitative estimate of the ongoing developments in carbon pricing around the world, which are otherwise not captured by the standard indicators of this report.

1.3.2. Revenue from carbon pricing policy reform

Current revenue from current carbon pricing policies

The Net ECR and Net EER indicators can be used to estimate government revenue from carbon pricing and energy taxation policies, including for different benchmark prices. To calculate total revenue from current carbon prices and energy taxes, each positive pricing component of the respective indicator is multiplied by the coverage base that it applies to, and then summed with the other components to capture all prices paid on the base.

To calculate net revenue, the sum is adjusted to account for free allocation of permits in ETS and fossil fuel subsidies (and electricity subsidies for the Net EER). Free allocation refers to the allocation of emission permits to certain entities or sectors without charge and are generally used to address competitiveness concerns for entities that are deemed vulnerable to the increased production costs resulting from carbon pricing policies. As this reduces the size of the emissions base subject to a price, it lowers the average price of permits in an ETS. It is also relevant to include in these estimates as free allocations represent revenue foregone compared with the auctioning of permits. Thus, to calculate net revenue, revenues from ETS are multiplied by only the share of permits that are auctioned, rather than total permits allocated. Due to accounting for free allocation, the net effective rates presented in revenue estimates represent an *average*, rather than *marginal* rate, as is used elsewhere in the report. In addition, the fossil fuel (and electricity) subsidies are subtracted from the respective effective carbon (and energy) rates and the resulting net effective rate is multiplied by its coverage base. All components are then summed to compute total net revenues.

Revenue potential from carbon pricing reform

The report then estimates revenue potential – the additional revenue that could be earned from raising the tax rates (or reducing subsidies) of countries' carbon pricing and energy taxation policies under different scenarios. This is broken down into several measures including: the phasing out of free allocation, phasing out of fossil fuel (and electricity) subsidies and setting a minimum Effective Carbon Rate. Benchmark values for a carbon rate follow the recommendations of the High Level Commission on Carbon Prices, which concluded that carbon prices must reach a level of at least EUR 60/tCO_2 to EUR 120/tCO_2 by 2030 (converted to real 2023 EUR and rounded) for countries to remain on track with keeping global warming to below 2 degrees Celsius (Stiglitz et al., 2017[6]). These values provide an indicative range of revenue potential if countries pursue their targets under the Paris Agreement using carbon pricing policies, noting that other policy mixes of price-based and non-priced based measures can also be used to achieve emissions reductions targets

To calculate the additional revenue potential from phasing out free allocation, the ETS permit price is multiplied by the respective emissions base as before, and then multiplied by the share of free allocations. The phasing out of free allocations is assumed to not lead to a short-term behavioural change. Calculating the revenue potential from phasing out subsidies and setting a minimum carbon price requires more steps to account for the emissions elasticity to carbon prices (i.e. emissions responsiveness leading to behavioural change). The OECD ECR dataset is used to estimate long-run elasticities (separate for OECD and non-OECD countries) capturing the responsiveness of emissions to carbon pricing.[2] The elasticities are then used to compute a reduction factor for the coverage base of the indicator, before being multiplied by the respective ECR (adjusted for phasing out fossil fuel subsidies or minimum rate). In this exercise, the reforms are implemented sequentially, beginning with the phase out of fossil fuel (and electricity) subsidies, followed by the phase out of free allocations and then raising the Effective Carbon Rate.

Revenues presented in this report are based on bottom-up estimations using carbon rates and emissions coverage and hence may differ from actual revenue figures collected by public authorities. In addition, the scenario analysis is an indication of the level of revenue potential from carbon pricing reform and does not represent a dynamic revenue forecast, which requires more complex considerations of changes over time in economic conditions, supporting policies, technological developments and behavioural responses, among others.

1.3.3. Revenue impacts from shifting energy tax bases in road transport

Section 3.5 in Chapter 3 includes an in-depth assessment of revenue impacts from the road transport sector's electrification. Assuming that every electric vehicle sold displaces the purchase of a comparable vehicle with an internal combustion engine (ICE), charging this electric vehicle with electricity also displaces the diesel or gasoline consumption of the replaced ICE vehicle. Such a counterfactual analysis requires taking into account differences and improvements in fuel economy across all vehicle types. Data on projected electricity consumption in the road transport sector and resulting displaced oil consumption is taken from the IEA's Global EV Outlook 2024 (IEA, 2024[15]). The IEA dataset covers for the years 2025, 2030 2035, the four vehicle segments, cars, vans, buses and trucks, while excluding two- and three-wheelers due to modelling uncertainties. Data is grouped in five geographical regions: Europe, China, India, the United States (US) and the rest of the world. Impacts on the revenue generation potential of specific taxes on energy use are estimated by applying Effective Marginal Energy Rates, aggregated by fuel and country, to the projected electricity demand and displaced oil consumption. The revenue impacts are then converted to shares of GDP using 2023 data from the IMF (International Monetary Fund, 2023[16]) and does not attempt to forecast or account for future growth in GDP. The analysis does not provide information on the impact on emissions due to data limitations on the carbon intensity of electricity generation and upstream losses of electricity and petroleum products (i.e. through transmission and distribution grids as well as pipelines).

References

Climate Watch (2024), *GHG Emissions*, World Resources Institute, http://www.climatewatchdata.org (accessed on 24 June 2024). [12]

D'Arcangelo, F. et al. (2022), "Estimating the CO2 emission and revenue effects of carbon pricing: New evidence from a large cross-country dataset", *OECD Economics Department Working Papers*, No. 1732, OECD Publishing, Paris, https://doi.org/10.1787/39aa16d4-en. [17]

Garsous, G. et al. (2023), "Net effective carbon rates", *OECD Taxation Working Papers*, No. 61, OECD Publishing, Paris, https://doi.org/10.1787/279e049e-en. [10]

IEA (2024), *Global EV Outlook 2024 Data (database)*, International Energy Agency, Paris, https://www.iea.org/reports/global-ev-outlook-2024 (accessed on 24 June 2024). [15]

IEA (2023), *Global Energy and Climate Model*, IEA, https://www.iea.org/reports/global-energy-and-climate-model. [3]

IEA (2023), *Terms and Conditions*, http://www.iea.org/terms (accessed on 6 June 2024). [4]

IEA (2023), "World energy balances (Edition 2023)", *IEA World Energy Statistics and Balances* (database), https://doi.org/10.1787/4a0c7aae-en (accessed on 8 July 2024). [11]

IEA (2023), *World Energy Outlook 2023*, https://www.iea.org/reports/world-energy-outlook-2023 (accessed on 6 June 2024). [2]

International Monetary Fund (2023), *World Economic Outlook 2023: Navigating Global Divergences*. [16]

IPCC (2023), *Climate Change 2023: Synthesis Report*, Intergovernmental Panel on Climate Change, https://doi.org/10.59327/IPCC/AR6-9789291691647. [1]

OECD (2023), *Effective Carbon Rates 2023: Pricing Greenhouse Gas Emissions through Taxes and Emissions Trading*, OECD Series on Carbon Pricing and Energy Taxation, OECD Publishing, Paris, https://doi.org/10.1787/b84d5b36-en. [7]

OECD (2023), *OECD Inventory of Support Measures for Fossil Fuels 2023*, OECD Publishing, Paris, https://doi.org/10.1787/87dc4a55-en. [9]

OECD (2023), *Revenue Statistics 2023: Tax Revenue Buoyancy in OECD Countries*, OECD Publishing, Paris, https://doi.org/10.1787/9d0453d5-en. [8]

OECD (2022), *Pricing Greenhouse Gas Emissions: Turning Climate Targets into Climate Action*, OECD Series on Carbon Pricing and Energy Taxation, OECD Publishing, Paris, https://doi.org/10.1787/e9778969-en. [5]

OECD (2019), *Taxing Energy Use 2019: Using Taxes for Climate Action*, OECD Publishing, Paris, https://doi.org/10.1787/058ca239-en. [13]

Stiglitz, J. et al. (2017), *Report of the High-Level Commission on Carbon Prices*, International Bank for Reconstruction and Development and International Development Association/The World Bank, https://doi.org/10.7916/D8-W2NC-4103. [6]

The World Bank (2024), *State and Trends of Carbon Pricing Dashboard*, The World Bank, https://carbonpricingdashboard.worldbank.org/compliance/instrument-detail (accessed on 10 June 2024). [14]

Notes

[1] China's subnational ETS is able to be modelled without the disaggregation of the national energy use data, under the assumption that the local energy mix is representative of the national energy mix.

[2] See reference for detailed information on methodology (D'Arcangelo et al., 2022[17]).

2 Pricing carbon: Developments in Effective Carbon Rates (ECRs)

This chapter offers a comprehensive overview of the evolving trends in carbon pricing including emissions trading systems (ETS), carbon taxes, fuel excise taxes and fossil fuel subsidies. The chapter highlights little change in emissions coverage and decreases in price levels captured by Net ECRs. Responses to the recent energy crisis have overshadowed increases in explicit carbon prices, while many jurisdictions are exploring the implementation of new or expansion of existing ETSs. In addition, this chapter addresses some of the practical considerations that countries are facing in implementing carbon pricing policies, including the choice of instruments, addressing cross-border emissions and pricing hard-to-abate industries, as well as the potential role for carbon revenues and public acceptability.

2.1. Trends in carbon pricing and coverage

2.1.1. Trends in coverage

Limited progress in the coverage of emissions subject to a positive ECR

Approximately 42% of GHG emissions across the 79 countries covered in this report are subject to a positive Net ECR – positive price coverage has not changed significantly from 2021 to 2023 (Figure 2.1). About 27% of GHG emissions in 2023 are covered by explicit carbon prices – an ETS, a carbon tax, or both - while the share covered by fuel excise taxes, an implicit form of carbon pricing, is 23%. Coverage by explicit pricing instruments therefore exceeds that of implicit pricing instruments, with a similar difference compared to previous years. Among explicit instruments, coverage through ETSs is much larger than through carbon taxes, reflecting the higher number of countries with this instrument in place. There are 40 countries with an ETS in place, compared to 27 countries with a carbon tax, and the preference for ETSs as an explicit carbon price continues to grow (discussed further in Section 2.2).

Figure 2.1. Minimal changes in emissions coverage of carbon pricing instruments

Share of GHG emissions subject to a positive price, in %, by instrument, all 79 countries, 2018-2023

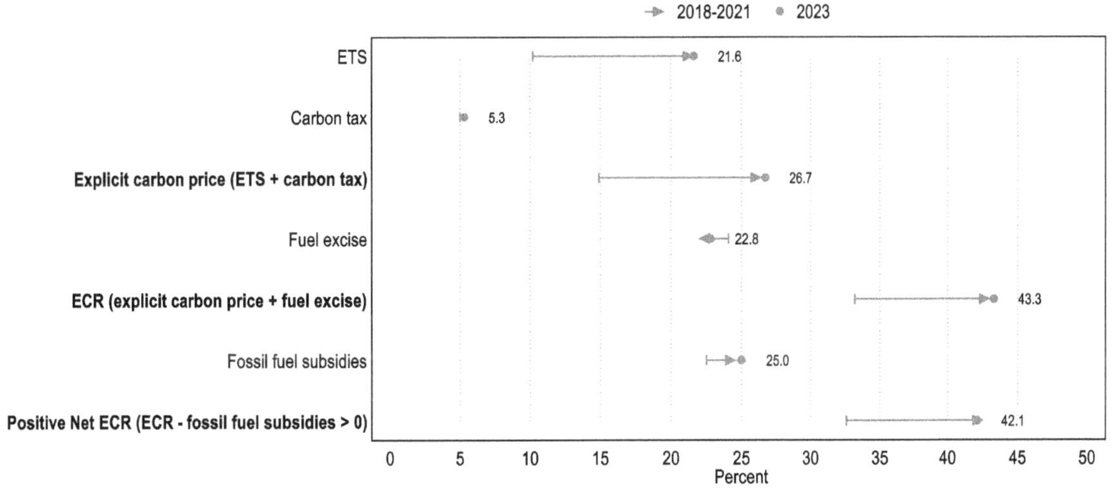

Note: ETS coverage estimates are based on the OECD's (2023[1]) Effective Carbon Rates 2023, with adjustments to account for recent coverage changes. Fossil fuel subsidy estimates are based on the OECD's Inventory of Fossil Fuel Support, where available, and original research for the other countries (Garsous et al., 2023[2]). Due to data limitations, fossil fuel subsidy estimates for 2023 are based on data for 2022. GHG emissions are the sum of fossil-fuel related CO_2 emissions, calculated based on energy use data for 2021 from the IEA (2023[3]) and other GHGs from Climate Watch (2024[4]). All 79 countries are covered for 2023, with varying country composition according to the coverage of previous editions in other years. Percentages are rounded to the first decimal place.

StatLink https://stat.link/cu1bfh

The emissions coverage of ETSs has increased by 0.7 percentage points and the coverage of carbon taxes has increased by 0.3 percentage points, accompanied by an almost identical coverage of emissions from fuel excise taxes from 2021 to 2023. These developments are mostly driven by only very modest expansions or no change of coverage of explicit carbon instruments across the majority of countries with the exception of Australia, Indonesia, Austria and Slovenia[1] which introduced new schemes. The largest change overall from 2021 to 2023 is in the expansion of fossil fuel subsidies, which increased by 1 percentage point from 24% in 2021 to reach 25% in 2023, strongly counteracting the coverage by positive price signals from carbon taxes, ETSs and fuel excise taxes.

At first glance, the expansion of carbon pricing seems to have plateaued. However, there has been modest progress in expanding the coverage of emissions within some sectors such as industry, while other sectors are beginning to be included such as waste incineration (Section 2.2). The focus among many jurisdictions has been on preparing for broader coverage and higher carbon prices and the consequences from these increases. This preparation involves addressing challenges in the administration and compliance of existing systems, addressing cross-border emissions (Section 2.2), as well achieving public acceptability (Section 2.3).

Stalled coverage hides underlying developments in carbon pricing

Among the largest changes in the coverage of positive pricing instruments is Australia's reform of its Safeguard Mechanism in July 2023, transforming it into a rate-based ETS through the introduction of tradeable permits (Parliament of Australia, 2023[5]). Indonesia also launched an ETS in February 2023, initially covering large coal-fired power plants, with plans to implement a hybrid 'cap-tax-and-trade' system with a carbon tax in 2025 (Indonesian Ministry of Energy and Mineral Resources, 2023[6]). Earlier in October 2022, delayed by three months due to energy crisis concerns, Austria launched a national ETS to cover sectors that are not included in the EU ETS (Austrian Ministry of Finance, 2022[7]). In addition, in July 2023, Hungary launched a carbon tax covering EU ETS participants that receive a proportionally large amount of free allowances, set at EUR 40/tCO_2 with retroactive effect to January 2023 (Government of Hungary, 2023[8]). Due to data constraints and its retroactive nature, this carbon tax is not modelled in the price and coverage estimates of the database. While the implementation of these countries' instruments may not result in significant increases in the average global coverage of emissions, these changes indicate progress is still being made in the implementation of new carbon pricing instruments.

Carbon pricing instruments under development

There is a growing number of countries with carbon pricing instruments that are under development, with a noticeable preference for ETSs. Instruments are considered to be "under development" if the government is actively working towards the implementation of an instrument, a mandate may have been established, but regulated entities do not yet face compliance obligations, and this has been formally confirmed by official government sources (The World Bank, 2024[9]).[2]

These developments include the EU ETS 2, which will cover CO_2 emission from upstream fuel suppliers in sectors not covered by the existing EU ETS (small entities in buildings and road transport sectors), which will take effect in all member countries (European Commission, 2024[10]). Türkiye has submitted an Updated First NDC with explicit references to a Turkish Emission Trading System and is developing a pilot set to launch in late 2024 (Republic of Türkiye, 2023[11]). Ukraine started the development of an ETS, for which it established a measuring, reporting and verification (MRV) system but this was put on hold due to Russia's war of aggression (Ministry of Environmental Protection and Natural Resources of Ukraine, 2024[12]). At the time of writing, the MRV system is in force but on a voluntary basis for participants. In 2023, Japan introduced the GX ETS, with the first phase based on voluntary participation by companies (Asia Society, 2024[13]). After the initial phase until 2026, the system is expected to transition to a mandatory ETS, combined with a carbon tax on fossil fuel importers from 2028. In 2023, Canada also began developing a federal ETS for the oil and gas sectors, currently undergoing public consultation with final regulations expected to be released in 2025 (Canadian Department Environment and Climate Change Canada, 2023[14]). Brazil (Feitosa, 2022[15]), India (Indian Ministry of Power, 2001[16]) and Colombia (Colombian Ministry of Environment and Sustainable Development, 2024[17]) have all developed national plans or legislation that establish the institutional and regulatory framework to introduce ETSs in the future. At the subnational level, in the United States, there are several states developing ETSs, including Oregon, Pennsylvania, New York and Colorado (ICAP, 2024[18]). In Mexico and Spain, the state of San Luis Potosi and region of Catalonia, respectively, are also developing subnational carbon taxes (ICAP, 2024[18]). The development of carbon pricing mechanisms across various jurisdictions indicate a growing global interest in market-based approaches to emissions reductions.

The share of emissions covered by a positive carbon price could increase by approximately 7 percentage points if the above-mentioned explicit carbon pricing instruments were implemented (Figure 2.2). There appears greater interest in ETSs than carbon taxes; the increase in coverage estimated from ETSs under development is 8.8 percentage points, compared to just 0.1 percentage points for carbon taxes. Several countries that are developing new instruments already have explicit carbon pricing in place at various levels of governance, including EU member states, Japan, Canada, Ukraine, Colombia and Spain. Taking account for overlaps between the emissions coverage of new and existing explicit carbon pricing instruments – whereby it is reasonably assumed that systems do not intend to cover the same emissions with two schemes[3] – results in a more modest increase in coverage for ETS of 6.7 percentage points. The estimation of coverage relies on published information on the instruments, combined with additional assumptions where details on the planned implementation are lacking. As such, these estimates should be interpreted as an upper bound of the expected change in emissions coverage (Methodology in Chapter 1). This modelling is an additional estimate and is not included in the core CPET database and therefore is not reflected in the coverage estimates of the Net ECR.

Figure 2.2. Additional emissions coverage can be unlocked from explicit carbon pricing instruments under development

Estimated Share of GHG emissions subject to a positive explicit carbon price, in %, by instrument, all 79 countries, 2023 onwards

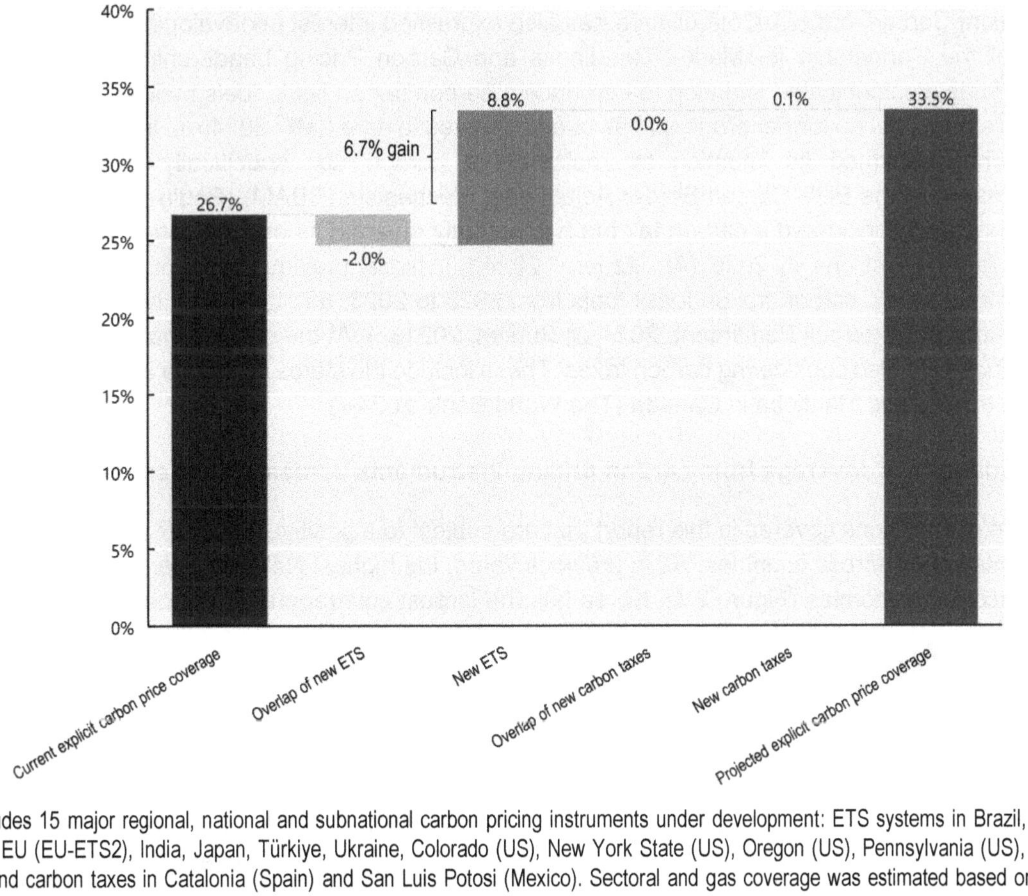

Note: Includes 15 major regional, national and subnational carbon pricing instruments under development: ETS systems in Brazil, Canada, Colombia, EU (EU-ETS2), India, Japan, Türkiye, Ukraine, Colorado (US), New York State (US), Oregon (US), Pennsylvania (US), Sakhalin (Russia) and carbon taxes in Catalonia (Spain) and San Luis Potosi (Mexico). Sectoral and gas coverage was estimated based on publicly available information, defaulting to electricity and industry coverage if information was missing. Note that final implementation details such as the threshold of facilities covered by an ETS, exemptions etc. can have a significant impact on instrument coverage. Thus, a middle estimate of 70% of raw emissions figures are presented.
Source: Authors' calculations based on CPET database. (The World Bank, 2024[9]), (ICAP, 2024[19]).

StatLink https://stat.link/slz8th

Carbon pricing instruments under consideration

There are also a number of countries that have carbon pricing instruments that are still "under consideration", categorised as such if the government has announced its intention to work towards the implementation of the instrument and this has been formally confirmed by official government sources (The World Bank, 2024[9]).[4] These instruments are not modelled above or included in the core CPET database due to a lack of certainty and details regarding their planned implementation at the time of data collection for these measures.

Among the countries covered by CPET, for ETSs, Argentina outlined a framework for an ETS for the power sector in an Omnibus Bill that was first submitted in December 2024, but this has been removed again in latest iteration (as of April 2024) (Padin-Dujon, 2024[20]). In May 2023, the Philippines conditionally approved a bill with provisions for an ETS and a technical review is ongoing (Philippines Congress of the Republic, 2023[21]). Malaysia has also communicated intention to launch an ETS but thus far only a voluntary carbon market has been introduced (Bursa Malaysia, 2024[22]). Nigeria also began discussions of an ETS under the framework of its Climate Change Act in 2022 (Manuell, 2022[23]). Chile has introduced the Green Tax Emissions Compensation System, although its classification as an ETS is ambiguous (Enerdata, 2024[24]). At the subnational level, there are also ETS under consideration in Maryland (US) and Manitoba (Canada) (The World Bank, 2024[9]).

Carbon taxes are also still being considered in several countries. Kenya's Climate Change Act shapes an administrative and institutional infrastructure for a carbon tax, but this is still under consideration (Promethium Carbon, n.d.[25]). Côte d'Ivoire has also expressed interest in developing a carbon tax in the context of the Partnership for Market Readiness and Carbon Pricing Leadership Coalition (2018[26]). Paraguay has communicated intention to introduce a carbon tax on liquid fuels by May 2025 as part of a series of reforms, but no further progress has been observed to date (IMF, 2024[27]). In 2024, the Moroccan government re-affirmed its intention to implement a carbon tax, specifically in response to the implementation of the EU's Carbon Border Adjustment Mechanism (CBAM) (Padin-Dujon, 2024[28]). New Zealand has also considered a carbon tax but has recently reverted its plans to introduce a methane tax on agricultural emissions in 2025 (Al Jazeera, 2024[29]). Israel previously announced its intention to gradually introduce a carbon tax on fossil fuels from 2023 to 2028, and has since begun implementation in September 2024 (Israeli Parliament, 2024[30]; Surkes, 2021[31]). At the subnational level, several states and provinces are also considering carbon taxes. These include the states of Colima and Jalisco in Mexico, Hawaii in the US and Manitoba in Canada (The World Bank, 2024[9]).

Changes in coverage from carbon pricing instruments across countries

The share of emissions covered in this report that are subject to a positive Net ECR through implemented instruments varies across countries. As in previous years, the highest Net ECRs tend to be concentrated in high-income economies (Figure 2.3). Korea has the largest coverage of emissions with a positive Net ECR at 99%, driven by the far-reaching coverage of its ETS, which has been gradually expanded since its introduced in 2015. As of 2023, seven countries covered in this report have no positive carbon pricing policies in place.

From 2021 to 2023, few countries implemented policies or reforms that resulted in a substantial increase in the share of emissions covered by a positive explicit Net ECR with the exceptions of Australia, Slovenia and Austria. Countries can increase coverage through the introduction of new carbon pricing instruments that are reflected in the Net ECR, or through broadening the emissions base of existing instruments (in the form of increasing the coverage base of positive pricing instruments or reducing the base of fossil fuel subsidies).

Figure 2.3. Across countries, changes in the coverage of carbon pricing vary in direction and magnitude

Share of GHG emissions subject to a positive price, in %, by country, 2021-2023

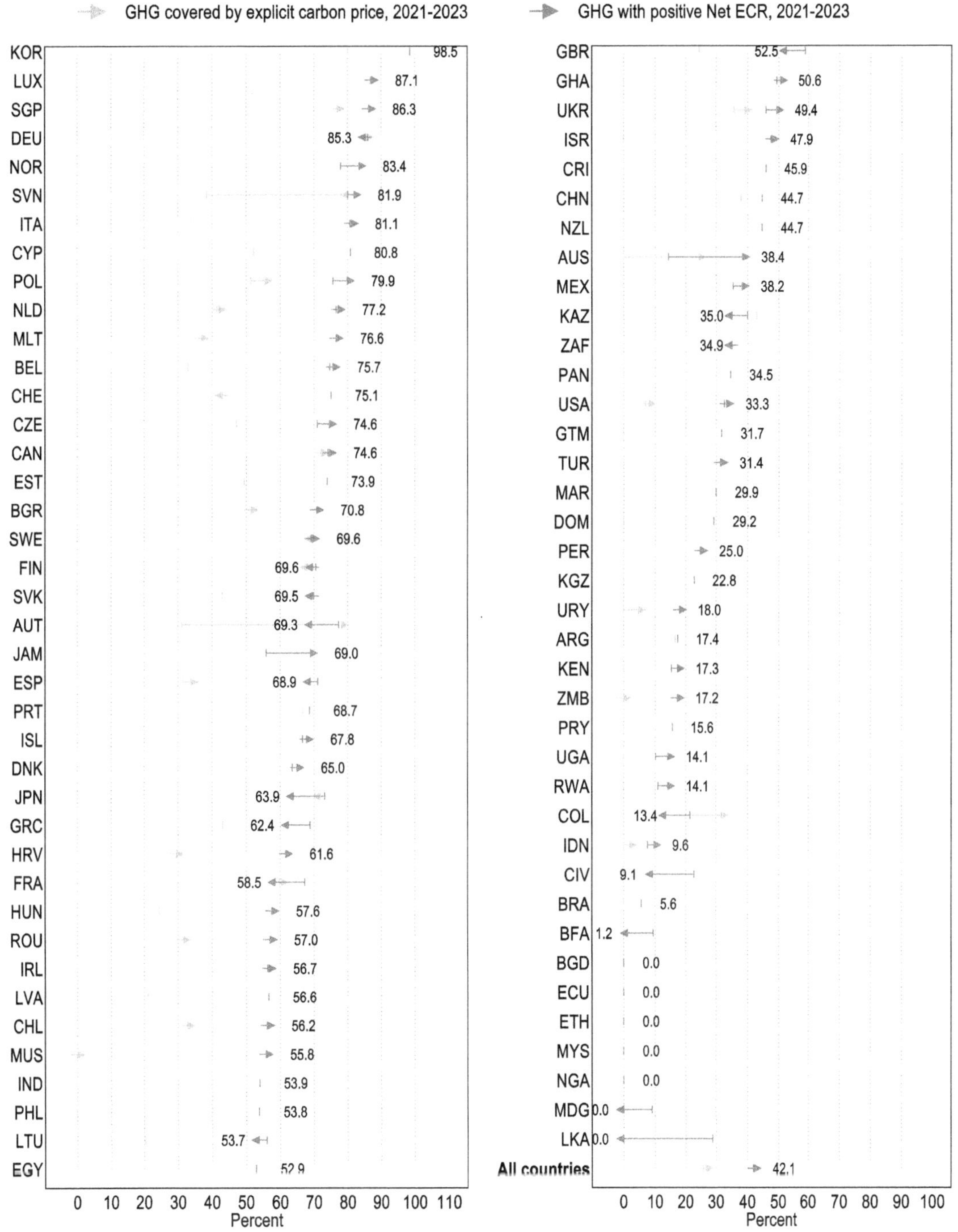

Note: ETS coverage estimates are based on the OECD's (2023[1]) Effective Carbon Rates 2023, with adjustments to account for recent coverage changes. Fossil fuel subsidy estimates are based on the OECD's Inventory of Fossil Fuel Support, where available, and original research for the other countries (Garsous et al., 2023[2]). Due to data limitations, fossil fuel subsidy estimates for 2023 are based on data for 2022. GHG emissions are the sum of fossil-fuel related CO_2 emissions, calculated based on energy use data for 2021 from the IEA (2023[3]) and other GHGs from Climate Watch (2024[4]). All countries are covered for 2023, with varying country composition according to the coverage of previous editions in other years. For newly added countries in this edition (Bulgaria, Croatia, Malta, Mauritius, Romania, Singapore and Zambia), there is no comparison to 2021 available and the arrow sign cannot be interpreted as such. Percentages are rounded to the first decimal place.

StatLink https://stat.link/rfmn21

In contrast to the modest increases in coverage, several countries faced a substantial decline in the share of emissions subject to a positive Net ECR. In almost all cases (except Colombia, Sri Lanka, Finland, Switzerland and South Africa), this was driven by an expansion of emissions supported by fossil fuel subsidies, reaching up to a 40 percentage-point increase for certain countries. In large part, the expansion in fossil fuel subsidies reflects countries' emergency measures taken in response to the energy crisis shock, starting in the second half of 2021 following the post-pandemic economic recovery and spiking with Russia's war of aggression against Ukraine in 2022. The ramping up of fossil fuel subsidies substantially outweighed the increases in explicit carbon pricing in most cases and led to a decline in the Net ECR.

Coverage of emissions continues to vary across sectors

The coverage of emissions by carbon pricing instruments continues to vary across sectors (Figure 2.4). The share of emissions with a positive Net ECR is highest in the Road Transport sector at 90%, followed by the electricity sector at 74% of emissions. In the road transport sector, fuel excise taxes as implicit carbon prices account for a large share of the coverage, whereas in the electricity sector, explicit carbon prices in form of ETSs are driving the high coverage. The sector encompassing other GHGs remains difficult to address through traditional pricing instruments such as ETS, carbon taxes and fuel excise taxes and therefore has the lowest coverage at 4%, although new efforts are being made to address these complex industries (Section 2.2).

The latest update shows that 58% of emissions are not subject to a positive price with the largest laggards in the buildings (67%) and industry sectors (72%), as well as the other GHGs (96%). Fossil fuel subsidies also have a critical role in accounting for the differences across sectors. For example, the share of emissions subject to fossil fuel subsidies in the electricity and buildings sectors is almost double of the share in the industry and road transport sectors.

On average, the share of emissions covered by a positive Net ECR declined slightly between 2021 and 2023 with some small changes across sectors. In some sectors, a decline is driven not by a decrease in the coverage of positive pricing instruments, but by an increase in the coverage of fossil fuel subsidies, particularly in buildings (subsidy increase of 10 percentage points since 2021), road transport and agriculture (subsidy increase of 6 and 7 percentage points since 2021, respectively). This primarily reflects countries' responses to rising fuel prices due to the energy crisis, which were targeted at the most-affected sectors. Notably, there was a modest increase in coverage in the industry sector due to new schemes and some expansions of current instruments.

Figure 2.4. Broad dispersion in the coverage of emissions across sectors remains

Share of GHG emissions subject to a positive price, in %, by sector, all 79 countries, 2021-2023

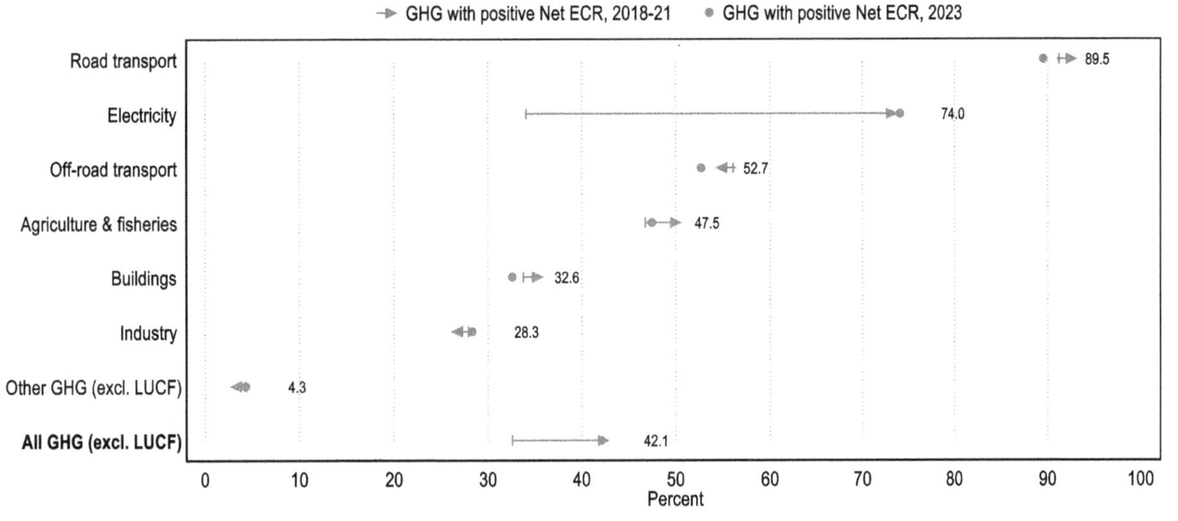

Note: ETS coverage estimates are based on the OECD's (2023[1]) Effective Carbon Rates 2023, with adjustments to account for recent coverage changes. Fossil fuel subsidy estimates are based on the OECD's Inventory of Fossil Fuel Support, where available, and original research for the other countries (Garsous et al., 2023[2]). Due to data limitations, fossil fuel subsidy estimates for 2023 are based on data for 2022. GHG emissions are the sum of fossil-fuel related CO_2 emissions, calculated based on energy use data for 2021 from the IEA (2023[3]) and other GHGs from Climate Watch (2024[4]). All 79 countries are covered for 2023, with varying country composition according to the coverage of previous editions in other years. Percentages are rounded to the first decimal place.

StatLink https://stat.link/vyh98e

2.1.2. Trends in net Effective Carbon Rates

Net Effective Carbon Rates have decreased, but ETS and carbon tax rates remained resilient

While progress in the coverage of emissions with a positive Net ECR has slowed down, the components of the Net ECR have moved in both directions. Ultimately, the decline in the average Net ECR across countries is driven by increases in fossil fuel subsidies and decreases in fuel excise taxes – reflecting emergency responses to the energy crisis – rather than changes in carbon pricing policy. Explicit ECRs increased from EUR 4.44/tCO_2e in 2021 to EUR 5.44/tCO_2e in 2023 (Figure 2.5). This primarily reflects the increase in the average ETS permit price, which rose to EUR 4.66/tCO_2e in 2023. In comparison, the average carbon tax rate remains much lower, at EUR 0.78/tCO_2e, having changed little since 2021.

As in previous years, implicit carbon prices in the form of fuel excise taxes represent the strongest price signal at EUR 11.73/tCO_2e, despite decreasing by EUR 2.5/tCO_2e from 2021 (EUR 14.23/tCO_2e). Given that only 48 countries have explicit forms of carbon pricing (carbon tax and/or ETS) in place and for many, at low rates, fuel excise taxes represent the strongest carbon price signal in many countries. In particular, low- or middle-income countries are less likely to have explicit carbon pricing instruments and rely more on fuel excise taxes. The change in fuel excise taxes was accompanied by an increase in fossil fuel subsidies, to an average of EUR 3.12/tCO_2e. Together, these changes reflect countries' responses to rising fuel prices, which are also evident in the decline in coverage of emissions with a positive Net ECR from 2021 to 2023.

Figure 2.5. A decline in Net ECR, driven by fuel excise taxes and fossil fuel subsidies

Net Effective Carbon Rates, by instrument, all 79 countries, 2021- 2023

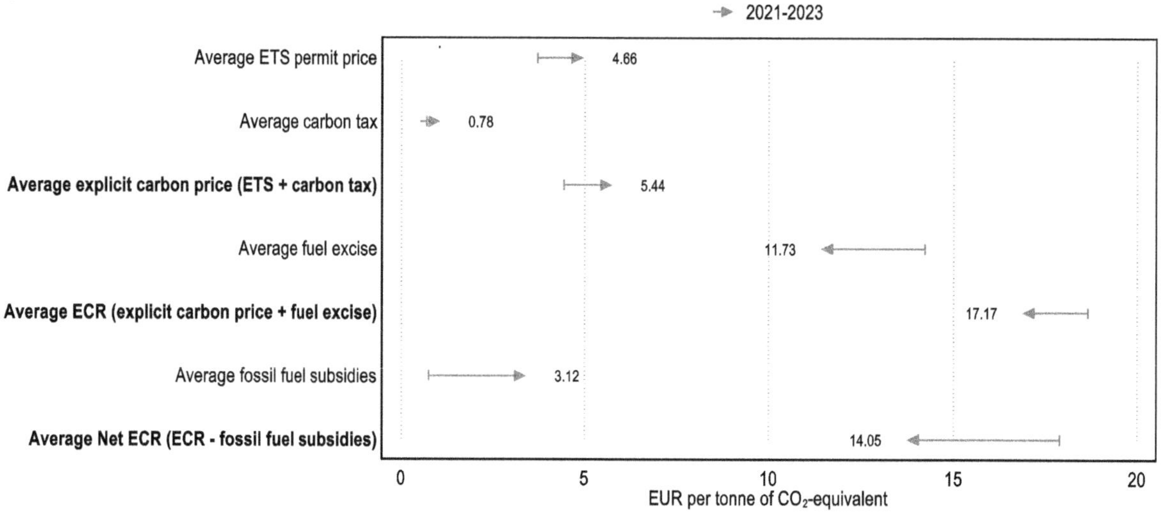

Note: Effective carbon rates are averaged across all GHG emissions of the 79 countries, including those emissions that are not covered by any carbon pricing instrument. Due to data limitations, fossil fuel subsidy estimates for 2023 are based on data for 2022. All 79 countries are covered for 2023 with varying country composition according to the coverage of previous editions in other years. All rates are expressed in real 2023 EUR using the latest available OECD exchange rate and inflation data; changes can thus be affected by inflation and exchange rate fluctuations. Prices are rounded to the nearest eurocent.

StatLink https://stat.link/1ktxg8

Recent changes to Net Effective Carbon Rates within countries

Net ECRs have increased notably – by more than EUR 5 – in six of the countries covered (Switzerland, Chile, Ukraine, Norway, Costa Rica and Canada) with some smaller increases in other countries, leading to an overall increase in the global average rates of both carbon taxes and ETSs. This suggests that governments have not backtracked on explicit carbon pricing efforts, but instead the Net ECR has been dominated by changes in fuel excise taxes and fossil fuel subsidies, largely due to the energy crisis. Some governments chose to tackle energy crisis concerns with different instruments, of which only some are included in the CPET dataset, such as fossil fuel subsidies and fuel excise taxes.

Other notable changes are reflective of large changes in exchange rates to the euro and inflation due to lack of indexing, such as those in Türkiye and Argentina, that can affect the ECR comparisons overtime. After the cut-off of 1 April 2023 for this edition of the CPET database, Türkiye announced a large increase in the fuel excise rate to compensate for this and to raise revenue, while Argentina has delayed fuel excise rises due to shortages in fuel and inflation concerns (Reuters, 2023[32]; Heath, 2023[33]).

Figure 2.6. Minimal increase in Net ECR across countries

Changes in Net Effective Carbon Rates, by country, 78 countries, 2018-2023

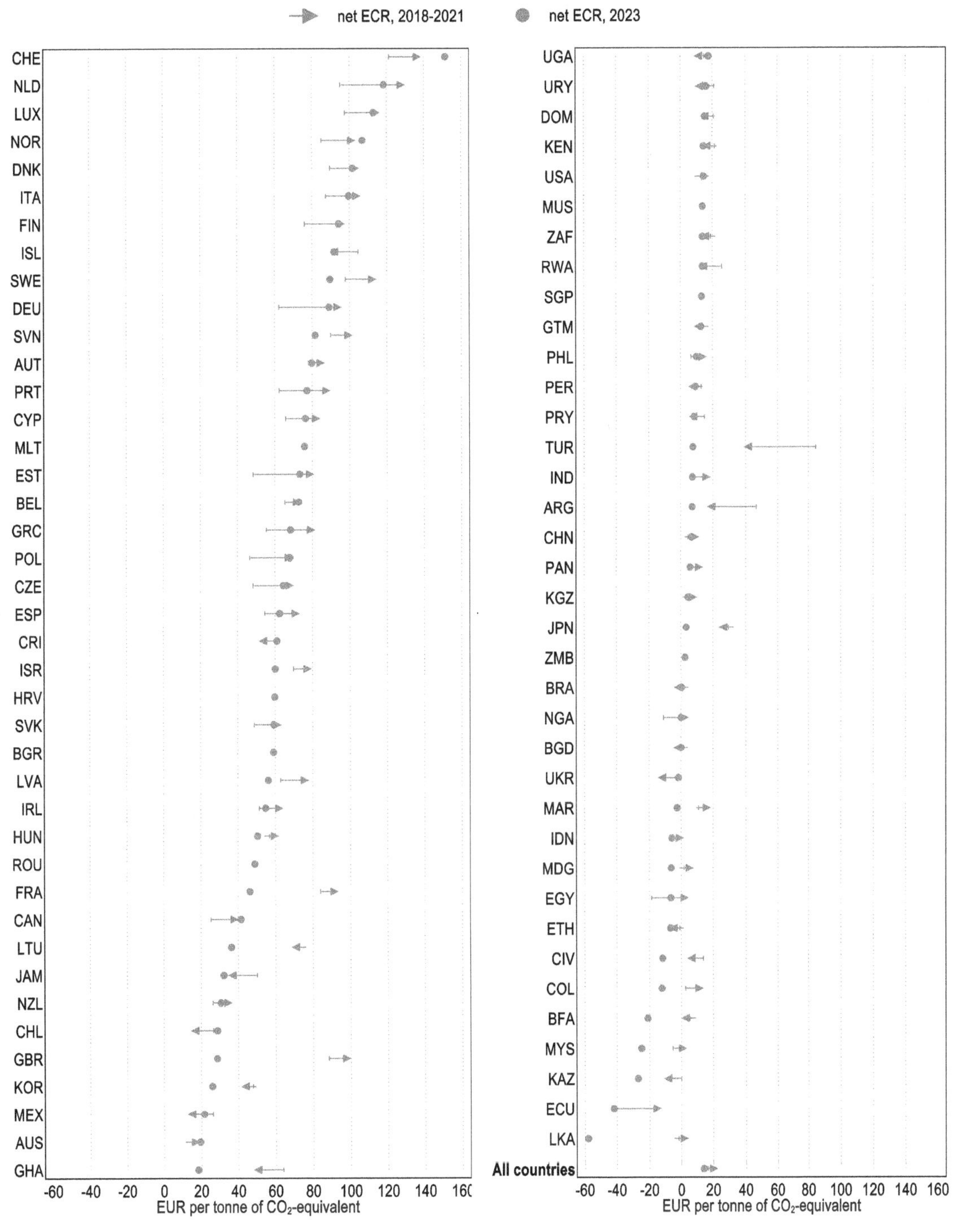

Note: Effective carbon rates are averaged across all GHG emissions, excluding LUCF, of the 78 countries, including those emissions that are not covered by any carbon pricing instrument. Due to data limitations, fossil fuel subsidy estimates for 2023 are based on data for 2022. All countries are covered for 2023 with varying country composition according to the coverage of previous editions in other years. For the newly added countries in this edition (Bulgaria, Croatia, Malta, Mauritius, Romania, Singapore, and Zambia) and the previous addition, there is no comparison to 2021 and 2018 available and the arrow sign cannot be interpreted as such. All rates are expressed in real 2023 EUR using the latest available OECD exchange rate and inflation data; changes can thus be affected by inflation and exchange rate fluctuations. Prices are rounded to the nearest eurocent.

StatLink https://stat.link/ar23m0

Although explicit carbon pricing remained largely resilient throughout the energy crisis shock, there were some countries that paused or reversed advancements on their explicit carbon pricing policies. For example, Austria delayed the launch of its national ETS, planned for 1 July 2022, for three months (Parliament of Austria, 2022[34]). Germany temporarily froze the planned annual price increase of its national ETS, keeping the price of 30 EUR for 2022 and 2023 (German Emissions Trading Authority, 2017[35]). Portugal suspended the planned increase in its carbon tax rate from March 2022 until the end of 2022 (Government of the Republic of Portugal, 2022[36]). Slovenia also repealed its carbon tax from August 2022 until May 2023 (Government of the Republic of Slovenia, 2023[37]). Indonesia, which planned to implement a carbon tax for the coal-fired power generation in April 2022, postponed this twice and instead launched in 2023 (Agung Swadana, Vianda and Tumiwa, 2023[38]).

In addition to changes in explicit carbon rates, there were also countries that increased subsidies to fossil fuels. Some emerging and developing economies, such as Ecuador, Sri Lanka, Morocco and Colombia, have long-standing subsidies, while others introduced new schemes amidst the shock of the energy crisis. These include France and the United Kingdom (UK) that spent upwards of EUR 40/tCO_2e on fossil fuel subsidies, followed by Lithuania (EUR 25.5/tCO_2e), Japan (EUR 19.8/tCO_2e) and Greece (EUR 18.3/tCO_2e). It should be noted that many changes have occurred that are not reflected in the CPET data due to ongoing revisions in support measures, whereby some measured have been discontinued and others introduced. For methodological reasons, the current fossil fuel subsidy data reflects 2022 measures.

Figure 2.7. Fossil fuel subsidies substantially decrease Net ECRs for some countries

Net Effective Carbon Rates, by component and country, 78 countries, 2021 and 2023

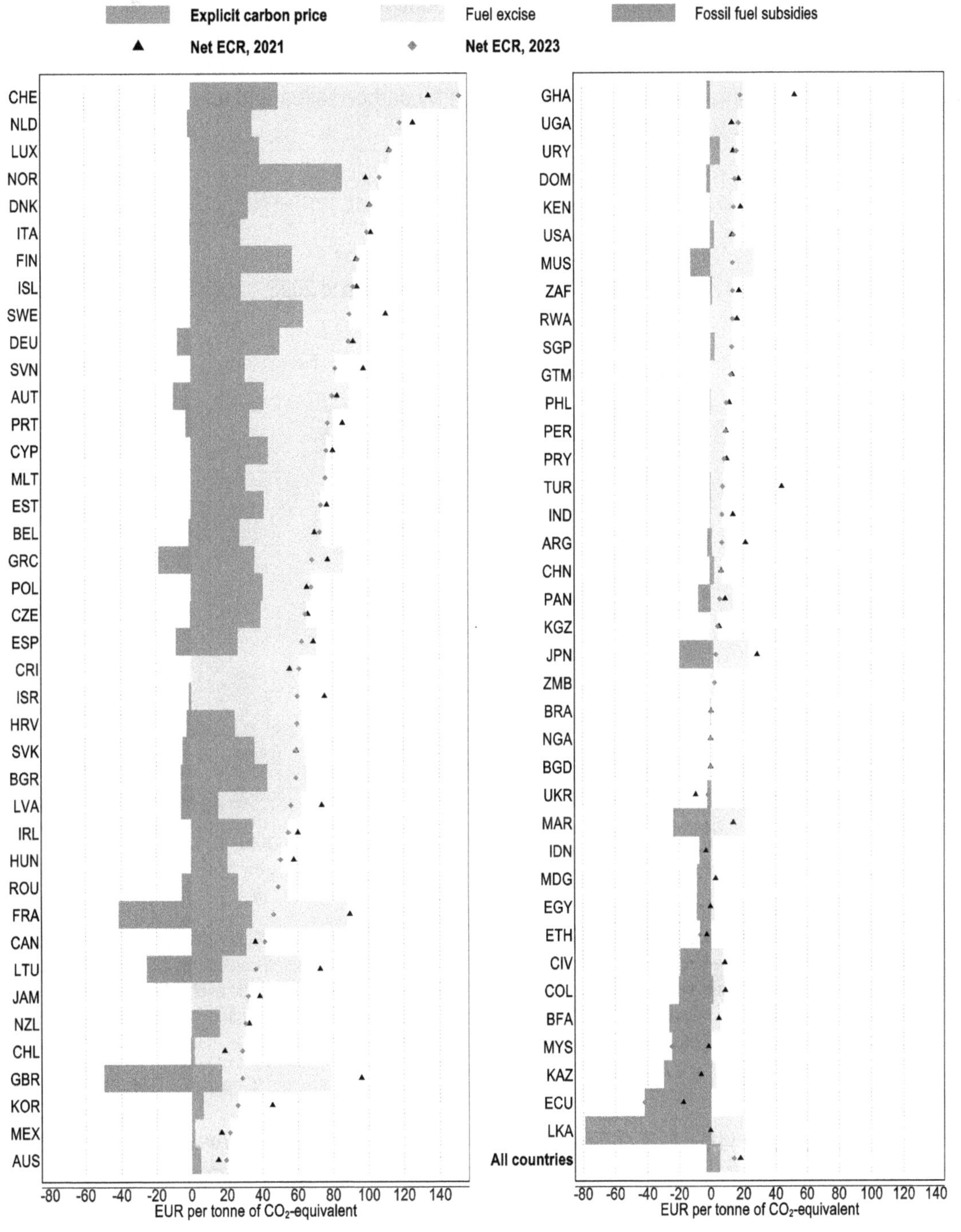

Note: Effective carbon rates are averaged across all GHG emissions, excluding LUCF, of the 79 countries, including those emissions that are not covered by any carbon pricing instrument. Due to data limitations, fossil fuel subsidy estimates for 2023 are based on data for 2022. All rates are expressed in real 2023 EUR using the latest available OECD exchange rate and inflation data; changes can thus be affected by inflation and exchange rate fluctuations. Prices are rounded to the nearest eurocent.

StatLink https://stat.link/w5joam

Net Effective Carbon Rates continue to greatly vary between sectors

The level of carbon pricing continues to vary substantially between sectors, with road transport continuing to have a Net ECR at least four times higher than other sectors (Figure 2.8). However, countries' responses to the energy crisis have brought about a significant reduction in the Net ECR of buildings, road transport and agriculture, while marginally higher explicit carbon prices increased the Net ECR of industry and electricity. This reflects the difference in instrument use across sectors, where emissions from the road transport sector and buildings are covered in large part by carbon taxes and fuel excise taxes and industry and electricity are covered by ETSs.

Figure 2.8. The energy crisis triggered substantial reductions in the Net ECR of buildings and road transport between 2021 and 2023

Average Net Effective Carbon Rates, by sector, all 79 countries, 2021 and 2023

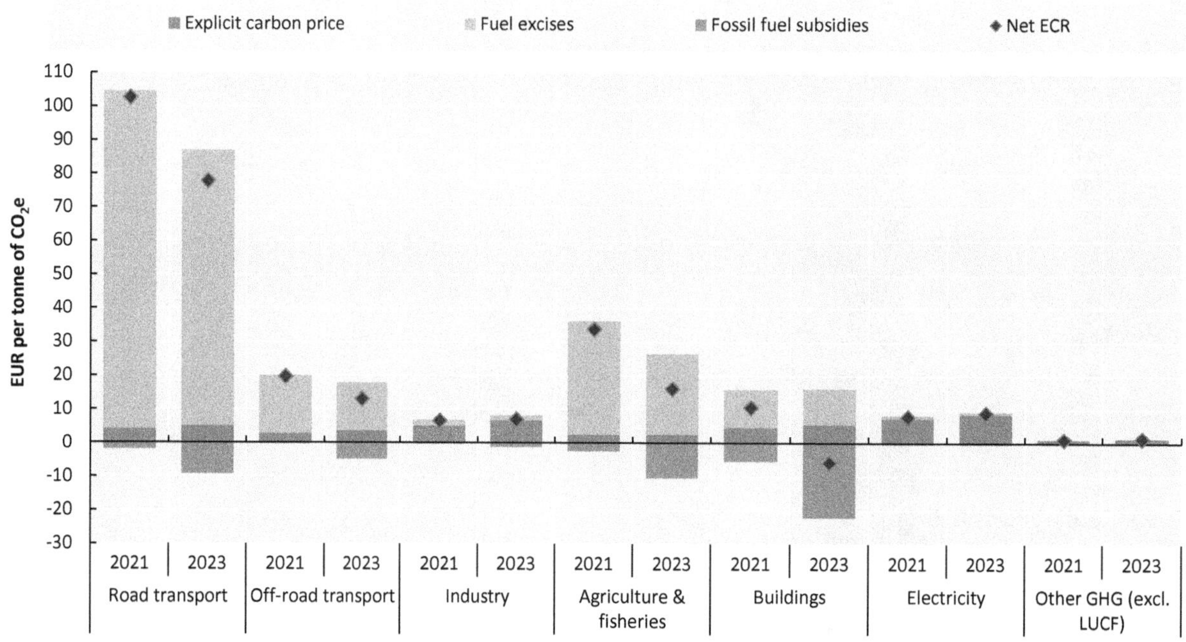

Note: Effective carbon rates are averaged across all GHG emissions of the 79 countries, including those emissions that are not covered by any carbon pricing instrument. Due to data limitations, fossil fuel subsidy estimates for 2023 are based on data for 2022. All rates are expressed in real 2023 EUR using the latest available OECD exchange rate and inflation data; changes can thus be affected by inflation and exchange rate fluctuations. Prices are rounded to the nearest eurocent. GHG emissions are the sum of fossil-fuel related CO_2 emissions, calculated based on energy use data for 2021 from the IEA (2023[3]) and other GHGs from Climate Watch.

StatLink https://stat.link/vifobe

In the wake of the energy crisis in 2022, governments significantly reduced rates of excise taxes on motor and heating fuels (e.g. gasoline, diesel or natural gas) and not all rebates were phased out by 2023. This strongly decreased the Net ECR in the buildings sector and to a lesser extent in road transport and agriculture (Figure 2.8). While road transport continues to face the highest Net ECR across all sectors – EUR 78/tCO_2e in 2023 – the rate is 24% lower than in 2021. Similarly, the Net ECR of agriculture dropped by 52% to EUR 16/tCO_2e in 2023. In both cases, more than 50% of the decrease results from lower fuel excise taxes. In addition to fuel excise rate reductions, many governments strongly subsidised households to mitigate negative social effects of soaring energy bills. This has substantially driven down the net carbon pricing level in (mainly residential) buildings. While the Net ECR of buildings was higher than the one of industry and electricity in 2021, fossil fuel subsidies decreased it by more than 155% to a negative Net

ECR of EUR -5.8/tCO_2e, the lowest Net ECR across all sectors. While fuel excise taxes dominated buildings' Net ECR in 2021, fossil fuel subsidies became the indicator's largest component, accounting for 58% of the rate predominately from a few countries – new measures in France, UK, Germany. Spain and Japan as well as expanded measures in Kazakhstan and Indonesia. The Net ECR of off-road transport decreased by 34% between 2021 and 2023 primarily driven by an increase in fossil fuel subsidies as well as the lowering of excise tax rates.

In contrast, the Net ECR of industry, electricity and other GHG emissions marginally increased between 2021 and 2023. Emissions in these sectors are more commonly priced by explicit carbon taxes and ETSs, where prices increased in the past years and free allocations have been phased down. Nonetheless, the Net ECR of industry and electricity remain at EUR 7.0/tCO_2e and EUR 8.9/tCO_2e, respectively. Other GHG emissions are also only priced at EUR 1.4/tCO_2e in 2023. Consequently, these sectors face significantly lower rates than road transport, despite each emitting more than double the amount of emissions.

2.2. Considerations in the practical implementation of carbon pricing

Recent trends in carbon pricing policies reveal a complex landscape. While the expansion of emissions coverage and price level increases have decelerated – and in some cases regressed – this apparent slowdown masks significant underlying developments that could facilitate the ramping up of climate action. To achieve the medium-term emissions reductions targets, a sharp increase in climate policy stringency, including carbon pricing, is essential.

There are a number of considerations government must take into account for the implementation of carbon pricing policies. These range from the choice and design of instruments, addressing cross-border carbon pricing in the face of international spillovers, and designing policies that are able to cover emissions in additional sectors such as waste incineration. These challenges help explain the current trends in carbon pricing policy and point to further efforts required going forward.

2.2.1. The choice and design of explicit carbon pricing instruments

Several factors can influence the preference for carbon taxes or ETSs, including administrative capacity, political feasibility, preference for certainty in price or quantity of emissions reductions and compatibility with economic growth. Overall, carbon taxes have significant practical, environmental and economic advantages, due to their ease of administration, price certainty and revenue-generating potential (OECD, 2023[1]). However, among countries that are planning or considering introducing new carbon pricing instruments, there appears to be a strong preference for ETSs. Eight countries are developing ETSs and another five have ETSs under consideration (Figure 2.9). In contrast, carbon taxes remain only under consideration in seven countries with none under development.

The trend towards ETSs could be a result of several factors regarding the design options for these systems. One factor may be that ETSs target emissions reductions directly (depending on design choice) by setting a cap on emissions, for instance. In addition, most existing ETS include free allocation of allowances, which can be used as a tool to mitigate carbon leakage or competitiveness concerns around emission-intensive and trade exposed industries and ease public acceptability (OECD, 2023[1]). This contrasts with most carbon taxes, except some that provide thresholds for applicability or exemptions for certain entities, as is the case in South Africa. Another factor can be the more recent interest in rate-based ETSs, which limit the emissions intensity of the system rather than the absolute volume of emissions (mass-based). Among the ETSs recently implemented in 2023, Australia and Indonesia both introduced rate-based systems. ETSs (and carbon taxed applied on direct emissions and not fuel use) also require monitoring, reporting and verification systems that are more amenable to linking with other ETSs and strengthen the integrity of carbon credits used as offsets.

Figure 2.9. A number of countries are developing or considering new carbon pricing instruments

Count of countries with explicit carbon pricing instruments, by status

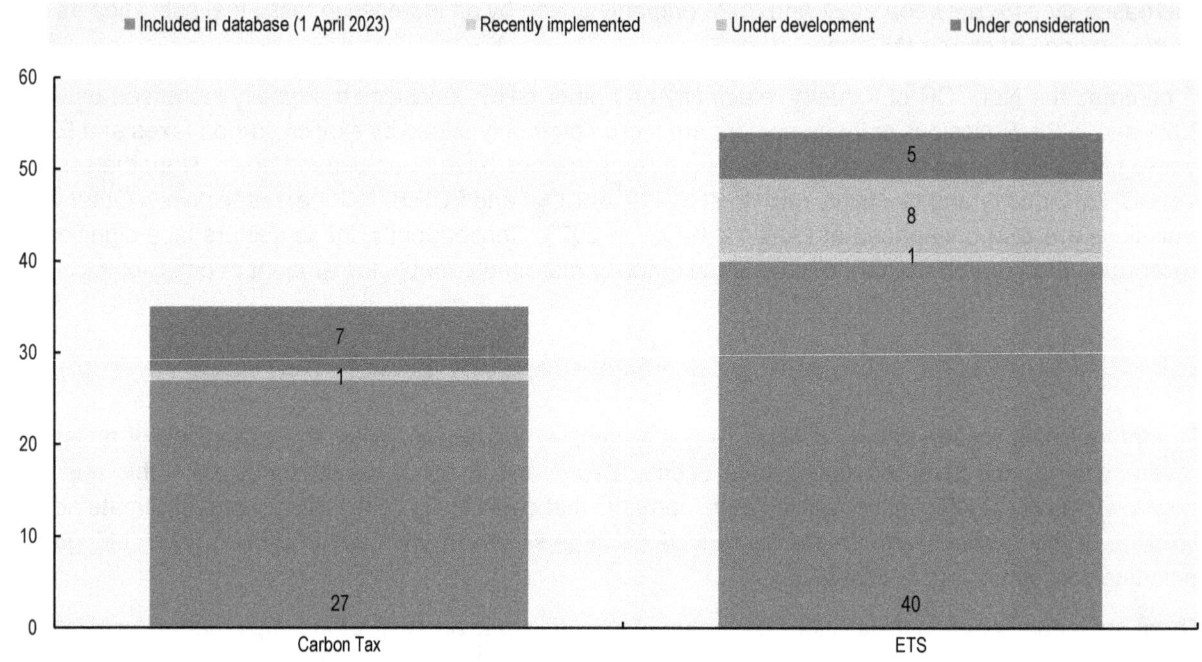

Note: The count considers instruments at the national level in the 79 countries (+EU) covered in the CPET database, as of 1 June 2024. Instruments are considered "Recently implemented" if they have been adopted through legislation after 1 April 2023; "Under development" if the government is working towards the implementation of the instrument, a mandate may have been established, but regulated entities do not face compliance obligations yet; and "Under consideration" if the government has announced intention to work towards the implementation of the instrument. Hungary's recent carbon tax is considered as recently implemented, although it is not modelled in the price and coverage data presented in the rest of the report due to data limitations.
Source: Authors; (The World Bank, 2024[9]; ICAP, 2024[19]).

StatLink https://stat.link/0dpqas

ETS have been shown to vary greatly in design (Fischer, Mao and Shawhan, 2018[39]). The two main types of systems are mass-based, whereby *total* emissions of an industry or installation are capped, and rate-based systems, whereby the emissions *intensity* is capped. In both systems, the cap can be declining over time. Mass-based systems include cap-and-trade systems. The largest mass-based system, by emissions coverage, is the EU ETS, while the largest rate-based system is operating in the People's Republic of China (hereafter 'China'). Among other countries, Australia and Canada have also introduced rate-based systems. At the time of writing, there is a mix between plans for mass-based and rate-based systems, among the countries that have ETSs under development and that have provided details on these design features.

There are numerous other elements that can vary between mass-based and rate-based ETSs. The additional considerations are the coverage of sectors, reduction factor of emissions cap, method of allocating free allowances, market stabilisation mechanisms and more, which result in a diverse array of ETS design. These differences, along with other elements such as the cost-effectiveness, ease of administration, scope and price predictability are key factors in choosing the best-suited carbon pricing instrument with respect to a country's domestic context.

2.2.2. Growing attention on cross-border carbon pricing instruments and international cooperation

Beyond design choices for domestic carbon pricing instruments, increased attention is being drawn towards tools for addressing cross-border emissions embodied in international trade. These emissions embodied in trade can be between economies with different levels of climate policy stringencies and carbon intensities of goods. Thus, the role of international cooperation and instruments such as border carbon adjustment mechanisms (BCAs) are being considered to help achieve global emissions reductions targets. Net ECRs across countries remain diverse, and although their dispersion appeared to be growing larger in the previous edition of this report (OECD, 2022[40]), this edition does not see the same pattern with only a handful of mixed countries significantly increasing Net ECRs (by greater than EUR 5) since the last edition (Switzerland, Chile, Ukraine, Norway, Costa Rica and Canada). In addition, there appears to be no trend in the reduction of Net ECRs with many economies decreasing Net ECRs across the spectrum of high and low rates.

Following the diversity of carbon pricing across countries, some jurisdictions are seeking a more targeted approach to addressing carbon leakage. The EU's Carbon Border Adjustment Mechanism (CBAM) entered into force in its transitional phase in October 2023. The compulsory regime that is set to start in 2026 will require importers to pay a fee on emissions associated with imported products based on the carbon price of domestic production. In its current phase, importers of covered products (aluminium, cement, electricity, fertilisers, hydrogen and iron and steel) must report the direct (scope 1) emissions and part of indirect (scope 2) emissions from purchased electricity, as well as some emissions embodied in relevant precursor products for complex goods, but at the time of writing did not have payment obligations (European Commission, 2023[41]). Starting in 2026, importers will be required to purchase emissions certificates for imports based on the differential between the EU ETS emissions allowances and the effective carbon price already paid during production elsewhere, accounting for free allowances and other forms of financial support (European Commission, 2023[41]).

In December 2023, the UK announced its intention to implement a CBAM by 2027 (Burnett et al., 2024[42]). Still in design, current plans present similar coverage to the EU CBAM, including scope 1 and scope 2 emissions, as well as select precursor product emissions embodied in imported products from the aluminium, cement, ceramics, fertiliser, glass, hydrogen, iron and steel sectors. The fee charged to importers will be an effective rate (similar to the ECR indicator) based on the price of emission allowances in the UK ETS adjusted for free allowances (therefore lower than the explicit UK ETS price), and the differential to other countries' domestic explicit carbon price (UK Treasury, 2024[43]). Further consultations are planned for 2024 to determine design and implementation plans.

There have been several proposals for BCAs in the United States, despite the country not having a federal-level explicit carbon price. The proposals and their various design features differ. The more recent proposal (re)introduced in December 2023,[5] the Clean Competition Act, would levy a charge on both domestic producers and importers of goods on the share of the good's emissions that exceed a sector-specific US baseline emissions intensity (Joint Economic Committee, 2024[44]). The Clean Competition Act was drafted to cover fossil fuels, refined petroleum products, petrochemicals, fertiliser, hydrogen, adipic acid, cement, iron and steel, aluminium, glass, pulp and paper, and ethanol starting from 2025, with expansion to other goods after 2027 (Sheldon Whitehouse, 2024[45]).

Box 2.1. The Carbon Rate Gap: a proof of concept using ECRs

A proof-of-concept analysis produces a new indicator, the Consumption Carbon Rate, using the OECD Embodied Emissions Estimates in International Trade (Yamano and Guilhoto, 2020[46]) and Effective Carbon Rates (OECD, 2021[47]) databases for 2018 to compute effective carbon rates paid on emissions embodied in trade, and hence on final demand. This is an effective carbon rate in final demand, following consumption-based emissions accounting. The proof-of-concept uses an input-output model to trace Effective Carbon Rates along the production chain, revealing the Carbon Rate Gap - the difference between the average rate on emissions produced domestically and emissions embodied in final demand or consumption.

The report provides first results that demonstrate that countries with higher production-based effective carbon rates tend to import goods for consumption from countries that have applied a relatively lower carbon rate on emissions. This results in more similar consumption carbon rates across countries, which could shift if border adjustment mechanisms are put in place or carbon pricing stringency converges. The proof-of-concept points to further analyses that can be used to inform climate policy decisions where issues of carbon leakage and other trade-related costs of carbon pricing have an important role. In particular, the methodology could be used to conduct counterfactual analysis, for instance, to model the effects of border carbon adjustment mechanisms on effective carbon rates, through the lens of complex global production chains that would add an additional indicator for the effects of these policy changes.

Figure 2.10. Carbon Rate Gap

Production-based Carbon rates less Consumption-based Carbon Rates, by country, 2018

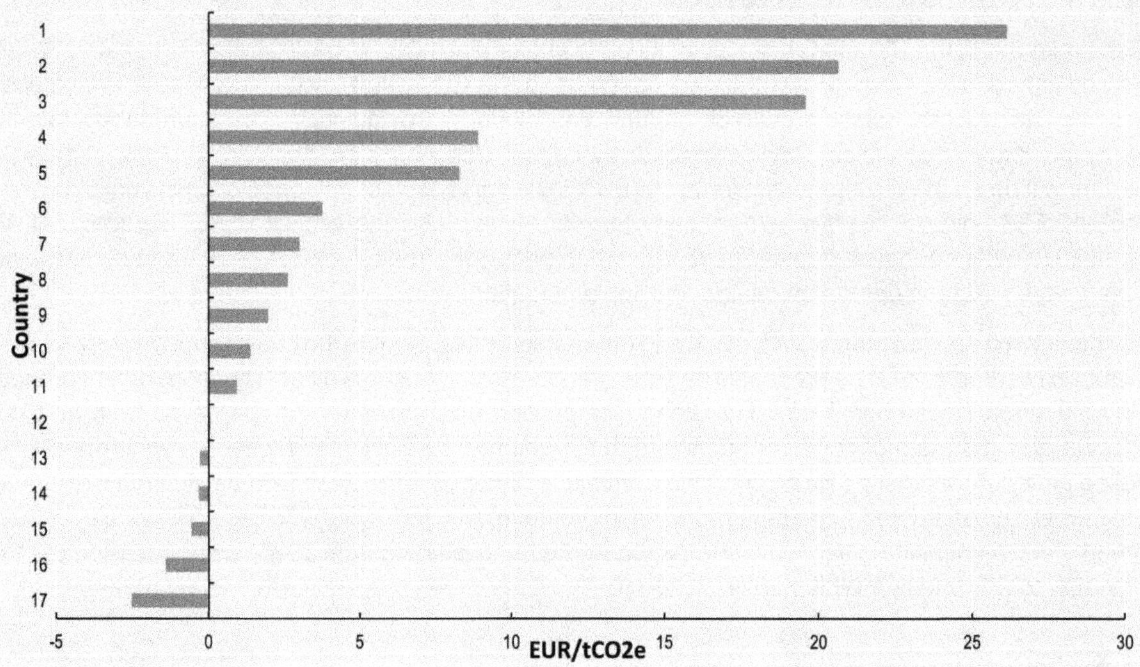

Note: Selected G20 countries, unlabelled.
Source: (OECD, forthcoming[48]).

There have also been new initiatives that aim at fostering global cooperation on climate change mitigation policies. In February 2023, the OECD launched the Inclusive Forum on Carbon Mitigation Approaches (IFCMA) (OECD, 2024[49]), designed to help optimise the global impact of emissions reduction efforts around the world through better data and information sharing, evidence-based mutual learning and inclusive multilateral dialogue. It brings together senior officials and technical experts from governments, as well as representatives from other international organisations, and is composed of 59 members (including all OECD members, the EU and 20 Project Associates). In December 2023, the Climate Club (2024[50]) was launched, a high-level forum for cooperation on the acceleration of climate action in industrial decarbonisation, consisting of 39 countries under the interim secretariat of the OECD and IEA. These initiatives mark growing effort towards global cooperation on climate change mitigation.

2.2.3. Practical challenges for sectors: The case of waste incineration

In addition to considerations regarding the choice of domestic carbon pricing instruments and new tools to address cross-border emissions, there are also practical challenges to implementing carbon pricing across some industries, such as waste incineration. Eventually, all carbon emissions must be drastically reduced through either pricing or other climate policy mechanisms. This section outlines the trends and practical implementation problems for the case of waste incineration, as an example of growing efforts to expand carbon pricing instruments to new sectors.

Waste incineration is a source of both energy and emissions. On average, the disposal of waste through incineration accounted for 29% in OECD countries and 19% globally in 2019 as a waste management category of plastics, making it the second most important waste management practice after landfilling (OECD, 2022[51]). Waste incineration coupled to a power plant (waste incineration with energy recovery) allows for the generation of heat and electricity. Countries covered in the CPET database generated more than 15 500 TJ from non-renewable municipal and industrial waste in 2021 (IEA, 2022[52]).

Taxes on waste incineration are generally used to recover the costs of waste treatment and disposal but can also act as a tool to internalise environmental costs and encourage behavioural changes. By increasing the cost of environmentally harmful treatment methods, it creates incentives to use alternative treatment methods such as recovery and recycling (OECD, 2019[53]). Among OECD countries, higher solid waste taxes are strongly correlated with reduced waste volumes and increased recycling levels (Matheson, 2019[54]). These taxes are generally charged on incineration facility operators by the weight of waste incinerated, measured in tonnes. Only a limited number of advanced economies have implemented taxes on waste incineration. While such environmental taxes are generally more likely to be adopted by governments with a robust environmental policy framework and a structured and monitored waste sector, they also require a country to operate waste incineration facilities, in contrast to alternatives such as open burning. Among EU Member States, nine levy a tax on waste incineration. Ordered by the highest minimum tax rate, these are Denmark, the Netherlands, Latvia, Belgium, France, Spain, Austria, Portugal, and Italy (European Environment Agency, 2023[55]). In addition, Norway introduced in 2022 a tax on incinerated, non-renewable waste.

As an emitting activity, waste incineration has recently moved into focus for climate policy. Advanced economies have started extending coverage of their ETSs to waste incineration or are redesigning their taxes on waste incineration. Integrating waste incineration as a new sector into an ETS or covering it with a carbon tax requires some methodological considerations.

Methodological considerations for taxing carbon emissions of incinerated waste

The redesign of waste incineration taxes and the activity's inclusion in ETSs impact the scope of both the Effective Carbon Rate and Effective Energy Rate. A waste incineration tax, levied on the carbon content of waste, is an excise duty levied on CO_2 emissions rather than on waste uniformly. Measured this way, this policy instrument uses emissions factors to approximate a proportionality between the weight of a specific type of waste and its energy and carbon content, effectively mimicking the design of a direct carbon tax. The impact of waste incineration activities covered by a carbon price on the ECRs and EERs implies two main considerations, its contribution to energy use and the precision of applied emissions factors.

The common method for estimating CO_2 emissions from incineration of waste is based on an estimate of the carbon content in the waste combusted, multiplied by the oxidation factor, and converting the product to CO_2 emissions. Volume 5 of the 2006 IPCC Guidelines provides methodological guidance for the estimation of GHG emissions from the waste sector (IPCC, 2006[56]). However, waste is a highly heterogenous commodity. Types of waste incinerated include municipal solid waste, industrial waste, hazardous waste, clinical waste and sewage sludge (IPCC, 2006[56]). The amounts of waste produced, their composition and their origin vary among countries as they relate to the structure of the economy and the level of investment in innovation and cleaner technologies. In many countries, information remains insufficient to monitor total waste streams, their recovery and the use of secondary raw materials in the economy (OECD, 2020[57]). This makes the estimation of precise energy content and GHG emissions factors for incinerated waste a highly complex and difficult task. This is in contrast to petroleum products where energy and carbon content of products are easier to determine and vary less across countries. Although not all countries align these fuel taxes with carbon content, emissions factors can be estimated by using default values. Increasing in precision as well as data requirements, these can be i) general, ii) country-specific and iii) incineration-facility-specific. To respect the proportionality principle between weight of waste and emissions, the highest possible level of granularity is required.

Two additional methodological considerations are needed when assessing how changes in policy instruments impact the scope of the ECR and EER. Adopting a carbon price on emissions from waste incineration, either through changes in design of taxes or the activity's inclusion increases the coverage of both indicators – but not by the exact same share. Following the IEA's World Energy Balances, the CPET database distinguishes waste-related emissions and energy use in four categories: renewable versus non-renewable as well as municipal versus industrial waste. However, the IEA's World Energy Balances only include energy generated from incinerated waste, that is, they only cover waste incineration with energy recovery across all four waste categories. In contrast, data on emissions also include non-energy related greenhouse gases. The CPET methodology stipulates that only non-renewable municipal or industrial waste is a fossil fuel that generates emissions. Consequently, coverage of ECRs only increases through taxes or ETSs covering emissions from incinerated non-renewable waste, while the coverage of EERs would be increased by both, the incineration of renewable and non-renewable waste but only where it is coupled to a power plant (with energy recovery).

Governments are expanding coverage of waste incineration

In the past years, multiple advanced economies have started extending coverage of their ETSs to waste incineration. This entails a change of the tax base from weight (measured in tonnes of waste) to carbon emissions (measured in tonnes of CO_2). Further, two OECD countries assessed in the CPET database have introduced or transitioned to emissions-based waste incineration taxes, Norway and Denmark.

In 2022, Norway introduced an excise duty on CO_2 emissions from waste incineration. The objective of the excise duty is to internalise the cost of CO_2 emissions associated with the activity. In 2023, the tax rate amounted to EUR 22.1 (NOK 238)/tCO_2. Since beginning 2024, the tax sets differentiated rates between EU ETS and non-EU ETS covered facilities, which stand at EUR 82 (NOK 882)/tCO_2 and EUR 16.4 (NOK 176)/tCO_2, respectively. The tax is calculated by multiplying the amount of waste delivered to an incineration facility measured in tonnes by a standard emissions factor of about EUR 0.051 (NOK 0.5498)/tCO_2 per tonne of waste. To incentivise sorting and recycling of fossil materials, incineration facility may apply for the use of a facility specific emission factor, if they can prove to the Norwegian Environment Agency that the fossil material content of the incinerated waste is lower than the assumed standard share of 55%. Incineration facilities that treat hazardous waste or capture and store generated emissions are exempted from this incineration tax (Norwegian Tax Agency, 2024[58]).

In 2009, Denmark converted its weight-based tax on waste incineration to one based on energy and CO_2 content to provide a stronger incentive to recycle the most energy-intensive waste. The tax is a combined input-output tax, charged via two elements: an incineration tax, levied based on the energy content in the input waste, which amounted to EUR 7.03/GJ (DKK 52.5/GJ) in 2022. This component consists of a tax on heat generated from waste incineration (EUR 2.77/GJ (DKK 20.7/GJ)), which is indexed annually with the net price index and an additional incineration tax (EUR 4.26/GJ (DKK 31.8/GJ)), which is not indexed. Further, a CO_2 tax is levied on incinerated, non-biodegradable waste which is indexed annually with the net price index (European Environment Agency, 2023[59]). This tax rate amounted to EUR 26.19/tCO_2 in 2024 and is scheduled to increase to EUR 95.23/tCO_2 (DKK 711.6/tCO_2) in 2025 (Danish Parliament, 2024[60]). Waste from biomass and processing of meat waste are exempted and an exemption for hazardous waste was abolished in 2010 (OECD, 2019[61]).

Waste incineration also became a core component in plans to expand the coverage of existing ETSs. If waste incinerators are included in an ETS, such facilities will have to buy emission allowances for each tonne of CO_2 emitted when processing non-renewable municipal or industrial waste. This additional cost of incineration can act as an incentive for waste prevention and recycling, which will then become relatively more competitive than incineration. At the end of 2022, the European Parliament approved the inclusion of municipal waste incinerators within the scope of the EU ETS as of 2026. EU member states must report and verify emissions from such facilities from 2024 onwards. It is estimated that the inclusion of municipal, non-renewable waste incineration in the EU ETS could decrease CO_2 emissions by 4.3 MtCO_2 by 2030 (Warringa, 2021[62]).

Germany amended its national ETS at the end of 2022 to include waste-derived fuels from 2024 onwards (German Federal Office of Justice, 2022[63]). According to a study commissioned by the German government this expansion in coverage would affect about 100 waste incineration plants, which incinerated 26.3 Mt of waste in 2019 to generate electricity and heat (German Federal Ministry for Economic Affairs and Climate Action, 2022[64]). By including this sector, Germany intended to close gaps in the emissions coverage and thereby create a level playing field with other power plants, which are already subject to a carbon price under the EU ETS (German Federal Ministry for Economic Affairs and Climate Action, 2022[65]). Likewise, Austria launched a national ETS in October 2022, which has similarities to the design of the German ETS. This system also covered emissions from waste incineration since its launch (ICAP, 2022[66]). Depending on the scope of the EU ETS after 2026, the EU system could supersede the German system in future (ICAP, 2022[67]). Austria already decided to replace their national ETS (Simon, 2024[68]). Furthermore, the UK seeks to gradually include emissions and energy generation from municipal waste incineration in its national ETS from 2026 onwards, but plans face opposition by local authorities which would bear the new, high tax burden after 2028 (Stefanini, 2024[69]; Stefanini, 2024[70]). Outside Europe, Australia's Safeguard Mechanism underwent major reforms in July 2023 that effectively transformed it into an ETS and waste in form of landfills is covered by the scheme (Australian Department of Climate Change, Energy, the Environment and Water, 2024[71]).

2.3. Promoting public acceptability and the role of carbon revenues

The next period of climate goals will soon require governments to significantly increase the stringency of policies targeting emissions, including but not limited to carbon pricing. However, an increase in the price level or coverage of carbon pricing may lead to additional burdens on households and firms and therefore requires a careful balance of achieving climate targets while addressing public acceptability concerns. There is evidence to suggest that both the choice of instrument and the use of revenue can help to mitigate the regressive impact of carbon pricing increases on households (see e.g. (Immervoll, Elgouacem and Raj,

2024[72]). Carbon pricing revenues could be used to create a 'double dividend' (see below), protecting vulnerable groups while achieving emissions reductions (Section 3.4 in Chapter 3) and transitioning tax bases from combustibles to electricity (Section 3.5 in Chapter 3). The political economy of carbon pricing – including trust in government, interactions with other climate-relevant policies, level of policy-relevant education among citizens, among other factors (Zhang, Abbas and Iqbal, 2021[73]) – varies greatly across countries. Therefore, countries are taking tailored approaches to design carbon pricing policies, as well as revenue use policies, that suit the needs of their economies.

2.3.1. Carbon pricing reform could unlock substantial government revenues

For some governments seeking to implement carbon pricing policies, achieving political feasibility and securing public support remains a critical challenge. Several studies and country experiences have demonstrated that the use of carbon revenues could help improve the reception of carbon pricing policies (Dechezleprêtre et al., 2022[74]). This may explain one reason why it is common for economies to earmark revenues from ETSs and carbon taxes for a range of expenditure areas (Cardenas Monar, 2024[75]). However, a range of factors can ultimately determine the political feasibility and public acceptability of carbon pricing, with economies choosing to earmark revenues for different reasons, such as budgeting for new policies and/or gaining public support. In economies where tax revenue use and the financing of other areas of public concern are prevalent issues to the public, earmarking can be one of several approaches that can be used to improve public support for carbon pricing policies.

Overall, the level of net carbon revenues (including revenues from positive pricing instruments, less expenditures on fossil fuel subsidies and free allocation of ETS permits) remains low, on average across countries just 0.6% of GDP (Figure 2.11). To compare, in OECD countries, public spending as a percentage of GDP was on average 5.3% on education, 7.6% on health and 16.9% on social protection in 2021 (OECD, 2023[76]). There is a large dispersion in net revenues from carbon pricing across countries. These differences can be explained by the higher levels of positive carbon pricing observed particularly in high-income countries, which generate larger revenues, as well as instances of very large fossil fuel subsidies expenditures, mostly concentrated in lower-income countries, which conversely lower net revenues. On the high end, net revenues reach up to 3.1% of GDP in Bulgaria. On the low end, several countries have negative net revenues caused by relatively high expenditures on fossil fuel subsidies that outweigh revenues collected from positive carbon pricing instruments. For example, Burkina Faso, Ecuador and Kazakhstan have net revenues of less than -2.5% of GDP.

Further strengthening carbon pricing –through increasing the price of ETSs, fuel excise taxes and carbon taxes, or reducing fossil fuel subsidies – could raise substantial revenues for governments while further cutting emissions. The exact revenue potential from a carbon pricing reform depends on prices, subsidies and several behavioural and macroeconomic factors that determine how the tax bases of instruments change over time. Nevertheless, an indication of how carbon pricing revenues can change, at least in the short to medium term, is useful.

Following the methodology described in Chapter 1, there is substantial revenue that could be unlocked from a carbon pricing reform that includes the phasing out of free allocation of ETS permits, phasing out of fossil fuel subsidies and implementation of a minimum ECR, ranging from EUR 60/tCO_2e to EUR 120/tCO_2e (Figure 2.11). The less ambitious reform of countries phasing out free allocations, phasing out fossil fuel subsidies and increasing their ECR to at least EUR 60/tCO_2e, would raise net carbon revenues to 1.7% of GDP on average. In the more ambitious scenario with a minimum ECR of EUR 120/tCO_2e, net carbon revenues would increase to 2.3% of GDP on average. This represents an almost quadrupling of the role of net carbon revenues in countries' GDP from today. For comparison, the median share of tax revenues (in aggregate across all areas of taxation) as a percentage of GDP was 35% of GDP across OECD countries in 2021 (OECD, 2023[77]).

Figure 2.11. Substantial revenue could be unlocked from carbon pricing reform needed to reach climate targets

Current net revenues, and total estimated revenue from carbon pricing reform (phasing out free allocation, phasing out fossil fuel subsidies, minimum Effective Carbon Rate), in % of GDP, by country

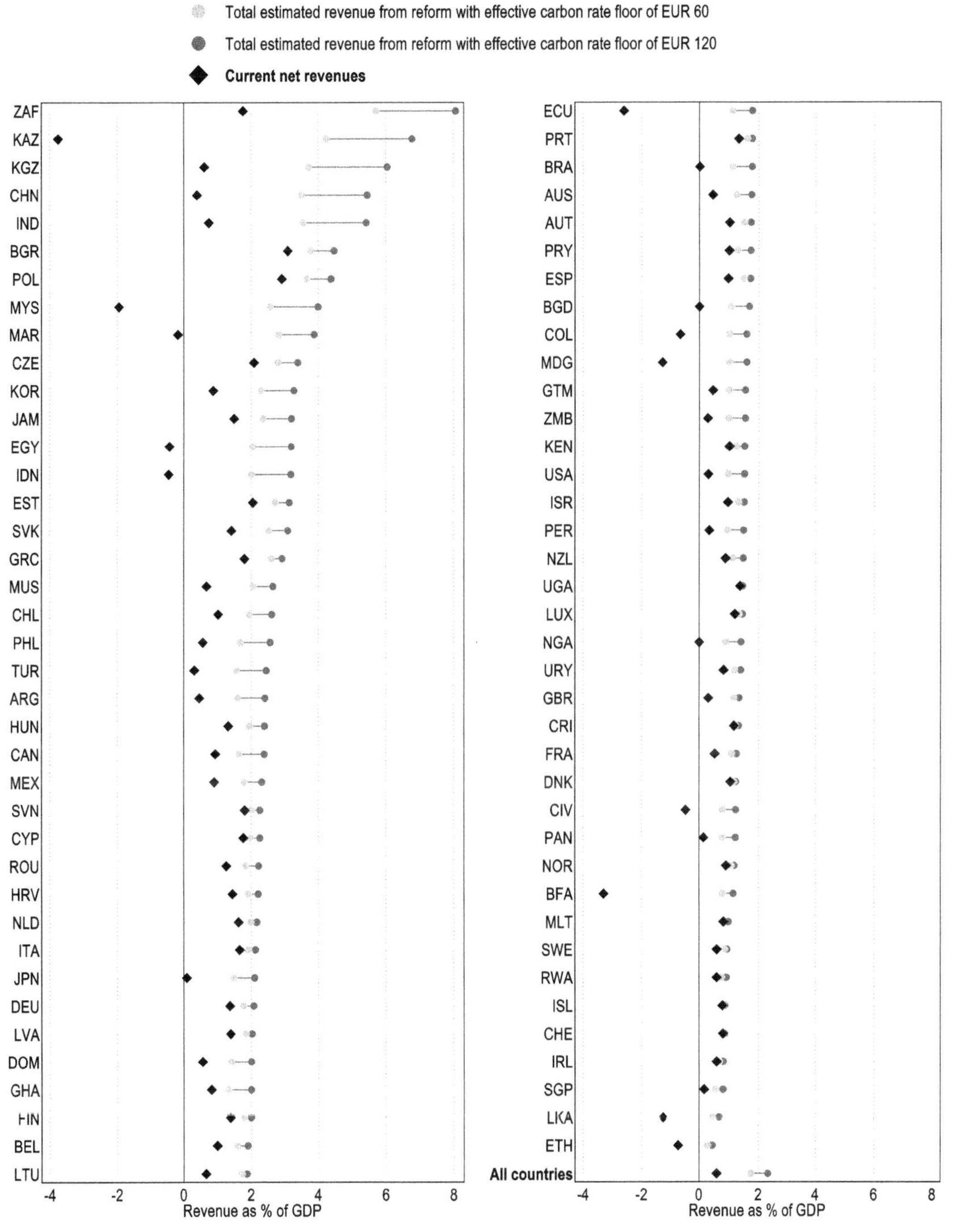

Note: Revenue estimates may be considered an upper bound of the actual revenue potential as they are estimated on historical data (fewer and more expensive low-carbon technologies, lower carbon prices, few developing countries in the sample). Estimates are for fossil fuel CO_2 emissions and do not include the revenue potential from reforming the pricing of other GHG or biofuels. Through accounting for free allocation, estimates are based on *average* Effective Carbon Rates, rather than *marginal*, as are used elsewhere in the report. Ukraine is excluded as an outlier to due to an exceptionally high emissions intensity of GDP, as a result of Russia's war of aggression.

StatLink https://stat.link/kml5qs

The revenue potential from carbon pricing reform is particularly high among a few countries, including South Africa, Kazakhstan, Malaysia, Kyrgyzstan, China and India, where net carbon revenues can reach 5-8% of GDP. In most other countries, the net revenue potential is much lower. Differences in revenue potential across countries to a large extent stem from pre-existing differences in countries' Net ECRs and for those with ETS, also the share of free allocation of permits, which tends to be higher in the earlier stages of introduction and phased down over time. Moreover, countries' emission intensity of GDP is a determinant of the carbon revenues as a share of GDP.

For some countries, achieving such a high carbon price may not be realistic, for many reasons. These include, but are not limited to, differing domestic policy priorities, focus on other climate change mitigation instruments, and lack of administrative and compliance capacities. It is likely that countries will continue to move at different paces, according to their domestic targets and capacities. Considering a lower benchmark, implementing a carbon pricing reform with a minimum ECR of EUR 30/tCO_2e would still raise revenues to 1.4% of GDP on average across all countries. For several countries, especially those that currently have negative revenues, this benchmark (including the phasing out of fossil fuel subsidies and free allocation) represents a substantial change in carbon revenues. In Ecuador, Malaysia, Burkina Faso and Kazakhstan, the share of carbon revenues in GDP could (as an upper bound) increase by 3-6 percentage points.

The additional revenue from a carbon pricing reform can be broken down to illustrate the components driving countries' revenue potential – including the share of revenue gained from phasing out free permit allocation, phasing out fossil fuel subsidies and raising the ECR to EUR 60/tCO_2e (Figure 2.12). The vast majority of revenue potential comes from raising Effective Carbon Rates (on average across all countries, 0.9 from 1.1 percentage points), with a much smaller role for phasing out fossil fuel subsidies and free allocations in comparison. This is in part due to few countries having ETS (and therefore free allocations), and on a country-specific level, revenue potential from phasing out free allocations plays a more significant role in some cases. For example, in Switzerland, Denmark, Norway, Sweden, Finland and Estonia, phasing out free allocations represents about 75% of the total revenue potential from the described carbon pricing reform. While different countries can pursue different strategies, depending on their national positive and negative pricing instruments, the overwhelming potential for unlocking additional carbon revenues is through raising effective rates.

Figure 2.12. Raising Effective Carbon Rates is key driver of additional revenue potential from carbon pricing reforms

Components of revenue potential from carbon pricing reform, in % of GDP, by country, 2023

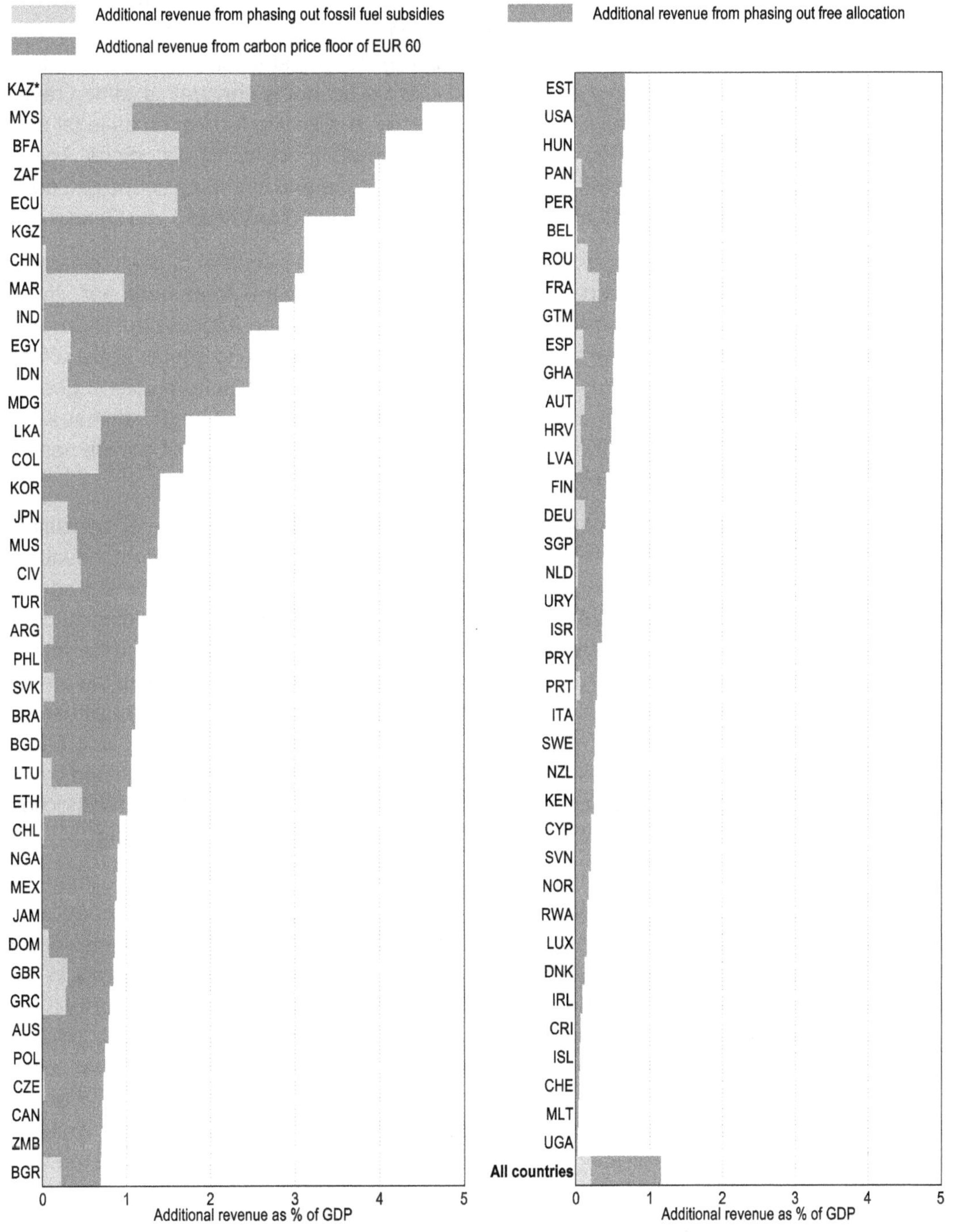

Note: Revenue estimates may be considered an upper bound of the actual revenue potential as they are estimated on historical data (fewer and more expensive low-carbon technologies, lower carbon prices, few developing countries in the sample). Estimates are for fossil fuel CO_2 emissions and do not include the revenue potential from reforming the pricing of other GHG or biofuels. Through accounting for free allocation, estimates are based on *average* Effective Carbon Rates, rather than *marginal*, as are used elsewhere in the report. Ukraine is excluded as an outlier to due to an exceptionally high emissions intensity of GDP, as a result of Russia's war of aggression. * The value for Kazakhstan is 8% and has been truncated in this graph for visual readability purposes.

StatLink https://stat.link/234zyw

2.3.2. Revenue use can serve as a policy tool to improve public acceptability

The revenue generated from carbon pricing instruments can be substantial with even higher potential if countries align their price levels closer to those needed to achieve their commitments under the Paris Agreement. While raising revenue is sometimes an aim and other times an outcome of taxes aimed at reducing emissions, decisions about the use of these revenues can influence the economic and political feasibility of these instruments (Barrez and Bachus, 2023[78]). The most efficient allocation of tax revenue is to a government's general budget in the absence of political economy constraints. When revenues are instead designated to a specific spending purpose – whether in a strong form such as legal earmarking, or weak form such as political promises – there is risk of creating economic distortions. This is in part because the connection between governments' sources of revenue and spending needs can be weak and can change over time, making it difficult to plan an optimal allocation (Marten and van Dender, 2019[79]).

While in general it is economically efficient to allocate revenues to the general budget, this does not rule out that there may be benefits to earmarking (in both the strong and weak form, hereafter), in addition to enabling tax reform when it might otherwise have been difficult or even impossible. There are various reasons for low public support for carbon pricing. The most prevalent relate to doubts about effectiveness, personal and collective fairness concerns about potential negative outcomes from carbon pricing policies (Maestre-Andrés, Drews and van den Bergh, 2019[80]; Carattini, Carvalho and Fankhauser, 2018[81]; Dechezleprêtre et al., 2022[74]), as well as public distrust in the effectiveness of government spending (Klenert et al., 2018[82]; Dechezleprêtre et al., 2022[74]).

Earmarking is one of several tools (among e.g. educational campaigns, stakeholder consultations and more) that governments can use to mitigate potential negative public acceptability consequences and improve public support for carbon pricing policies. Existing studies demonstrate that individuals have a strong preference for earmarking revenues from carbon taxes for environmental spending, such as further emissions reduction efforts (Carattini, Carvalho and Fankhauser, 2018[81]; Baranzini and Carattini, 2017[83]; Maestre-Andrés, Drews and van den Bergh, 2019[80]). This may be due to doubts about the environmental effectiveness of the tax, therefore warranting additional environmental spending (Baranzini and Carattini, 2017[83]), as well as a psychological preference for thematic matching between the source and spending of the revenues (Mus, Mercierid and Chevallierid, 2023[84]). In addition, a survey conducted by the OECD (Dechezleprêtre et al., 2022[74]) suggests that effective communication to explain the functioning and distributional outcomes of policies can increase stated political support for carbon pricing.

Indeed, revenues from explicit pricing, and in particular ETSs, are most often used for climate change or related environmental purposes (Fleurence, Fetet and Postic, 2023[85]). Often, revenues are used to finance investments in additional sectors that are not covered by the carbon pricing policies and serve as complementary to the carbon price. These measures can include for instance, investments in low-carbon technologies, expansion of green transport infrastructure, biodiversity protection and more (in the EU, for instance, Member States are mandated to spend at least 50% of ETS auction revenues for climate- and energy-related purposes (European Commission, 2024[86]). However, climate-related spending is not the only, or necessarily most optimal, area for expenditure (Table 2.1). The most effective form of earmarking will be unique to each country and dependent on a number of factors, including but not limited to public concerns, the existing tax system, existing sustainable development related policies, and the vulnerability of businesses and households to higher carbon prices.

Existing studies demonstrate that revenue use tends to also differ by instrument type (Marten and van Dender, 2019[79]). While revenues from excise taxes – which make up the dominant share – tend to remain in the general budget, revenues from ETSs and carbon taxes are more commonly earmarked (both in the strong and weak form). In addition, constraints on excise taxes revenue, when used, tend to be applied to fuels used for specific purposes (e.g., automotive fuels), whereas constraints on revenues from ETSs and carbon taxes more often cover all revenue.

Table 2.1. Uses of carbon pricing revenues go beyond environmental/climate objectives

Overview of types of uses of carbon pricing revenues

Type	Description	Example
Tax reform	The broader tax system is reformed to lower the rate of tax levied on personal or business income with the aim of boosting economic growth through reducing tax distortions caused by disincentives to labour market participation, consumption and investment. This is also used to offset the potential negative effects of lower real wages in response to higher prices, stemming from the increase in carbon pricing.	British Columbia's carbon tax was introduced in 2008 alongside additional tax reforms, including cuts to personal and corporate income taxes. The tax reforms were designed to create a revenue-neutral carbon tax, meaning costs imposed on households and businesses from higher carbon prices would be offset by a reduction in other taxes (Government of British Columbia, 2024[87])
Compensation to households and firms	Compensation measures are given to alleviate negative impacts from higher carbon pricing in the form of higher electricity and fuel prices, as well as a loss of employment in emission-intensive industries. These measures can be in the form of direct cash transfers, subsidies or other relief measures such as support for occupational retraining. They may be distributed universally or to particular regions, sectors or income groups that face a disproportionate burden.	Austria's Klimabonus is an annual cash transfer made to all main residents of Austria as direct compensation for, and funded by, its carbon tax that was introduced in 2022. In 2023, the base amount (subject to an additional regional allowance) equaled EUR 110 (Government of Austria, n.d.[88])
Prevention of competitiveness and carbon leakage effects	This addresses international competitiveness concerns in particular for emissions-intensive and trade-exposed firms that have difficulties to reduce the carbon intensity of their production in the short- or long-term and may be at risk of carbon leakage. These measures can be in the form of free allocation of allowances in ETS, partial tax exemptions or feebates to reduce the cost of compliance with carbon pricing policies for firms	South Africa's carbon tax, introduced in 2019, contains a number of tax-free allowances to account for competitiveness concerns, particularly for emissions-intensive and trade-exposed sectors. For example, trade-exposed sectors receive a tax allowance up to maximum 10%, based on a measure of their trade exposure (South African Revenue Service, n.d.[89])
Other development objectives	Revenues can be contributed to funds for sustainable development policies, including for example spending on health, education, infrastructure projects such as public transport, and more. This is often done as part of a policy package targeting interlinkages between environmental, social and economic development	The California Climate Investments is a set of programmes across a range of sustainable development areas, funded by the state's ETS revenues. In the first half of 2023, 84% of revenues benefitted 'priority populations' (disadvantaged and low-income communities) through projects such as low-carbon transit, air quality monitoring, and solar power for schools and community centres (California Climate Investments, n.d.[90])

Note: Examples are not exhaustive.
Source: Authors & (World Bank, 2019[91]).

As mentioned, raising the stringency of carbon pricing carries an economic burden, and earmarking could have an influence on the public support of carbon pricing policies. Different uses of revenues have their individual considerations regarding their administrative burden, impact on economic efficiency and political feasibility of the revenue use itself, among other factors (Black, Zhunussova and Parry, 2022[92]). Decisions about how and where to allocate carbon revenues require careful consideration of these factors, countries' economic and political landscapes, as well as the potential advantages and disadvantages of earmarking more broadly. In addition, there are several other policy tools that governments may choose to use in addition to, or instead of, earmarking to raise public support.

Earmarking can be used to mitigate potential negative effects of carbon pricing policies, that as any other taxes, may improve environmental outcomes but reduce overall economic benefits. It can also be used to connect climate targets to other important (potentially different) areas of public concern. In addition, earmarking can provide greater transparency about policy instruments for taxpayers. However, there are also some potential disadvantages. For instance, if earmarking results in insufficient or excess tax revenue for a particular cause, this can result in under- or over-investment in that area, distorting the optimal spending outcomes and reducing the overall efficiency of the tax system. Governments that choose to earmark revenues will also have reduced flexibility with expenditures to respond to changing priorities or unforeseen circumstances. In addition, in general, allocating revenues to the general budget may be administratively simpler and more flexible than earmarking. Some countries may even have legal constraints to earmarking. Finally, the public visibility of earmarked expenditures may influence intended outcomes, specifically for the case of facilitating public support for policies through earmarking.

Ultimately, countries will choose differing approaches to carbon pricing, as well as the use of carbon revenues as a related policy instrument. A flexible approach whereby countries are able to design their policy instruments, such as earmarking, based on their individual policy priorities and policy landscape can help maintain the momentum needed to achieve approaching climate targets both in terms of political feasibility and public acceptance.

References

Agung Swadana, W., F. Vianda and F. Tumiwa (2023), *Navigating Indonesia's Carbon Market: Challenges, Opportunities, and the Road Ahead*, Institute for Essential Services Reform, https://iesr.or.id/en/navigating-indonesias-carbon-market-challenges-opportunities-and-the-road-ahead (accessed on 6 June 2024). [38]

Al Jazeera (2024), *New Zealand scraps 'burp tax' on livestock after backlash from farmers*, Al Jazeera Media Network, https://www.aljazeera.com/economy/2024/6/11/new-zealand-scraps-burp-tax-on-livestock-after-backlash-from-farmers (accessed on 21 June 2024). [29]

Asia Society (2024), *ETS Status: Japan GX-ETS (National Voluntary ETS)*, Asia Society, https://asiasociety.org/policy-institute/ets-status-japan (accessed on 20 June 2024). [13]

Australian Department of Climate Change, Energy, the Environment and Water (2024), *Safeguard Mechanism*, https://www.dcceew.gov.au/climate-change/emissions-reporting/national-greenhouse-energy-reporting-scheme/safeguard-mechanism (accessed on 24 June 2024). [71]

Austrian Ministry of Finance (2022), *Nationales Emissionszertifikatehandelsgesetz 2022 [National Emissions Trading Act 2022]*, Austria Ministry of Finance, https://www.bmf.gv.at/themen/klimapolitik/carbon-markets/nationales-emissionszertifikatehandelsgesetz-2022-(NEHG-2022).html (accessed on 20 June 2024). [7]

Baranzini, A. and S. Carattini (2017), "Effectiveness, earmarking and labeling: testing the acceptability of carbon taxes with survey data", *Environmental Economics and Policy Studies*, Vol. 19/1, pp. 197-227, https://doi.org/10.1007/S10018-016-0144-7/TABLES/5. [83]

Barrez, J. and K. Bachus (2023), "Public acceptability of carbon pricing: A literature review", *Equity, Efficiency and Acceptability of Carbon Pricing in Belgium*, KU Leuven, Leuven, http://hiva.kuleuven.be (accessed on 16 July 2024). [78]

Black, S., K. Zhunussova and I. Parry (2022), "Carbon Taxes or Emissions Trading Systems?", *Staff Climate Notes*, Vol. 2022/006, p. 1, https://doi.org/10.5089/9798400212307.066. [92]

Burnett, N. et al. (2024), *Carbon Border Adjustment Mechanism*, UK Parliament House of Commons Library, https://commonslibrary.parliament.uk/research-briefings/cbp-9935/ (accessed on 21 June 2024). [42]

Bursa Malaysia (2024), *Voluntary Carbon Market Exchange*, Bursa Malaysia, https://www.bursamalaysia.com/trade/market/voluntary-carbon-market-exchange/overview (accessed on 21 June 2024). [22]

California Climate Investments (n.d.), *Priority Populations*, California Climate Investments, https://www.caclimateinvestments.ca.gov/priority-populations (accessed on 6 June 2024). [90]

Canadian Department Environment and Climate Change Canada (2023), *A Regulatory Framework To Cap Oil and Gas Sector Greenhouse Gas Emissions*, His Majesty the King in Right of Canada, represented by the Minister of Environment and Climate Change, https://publications.gc.ca/site/eng/9.930861/publication.html (accessed on 20 June 2024). [14]

Carattini, S., M. Carvalho and S. Fankhauser (2018), "Overcoming public resistance to carbon taxes", *Wiley Interdisciplinary Reviews: Climate Change*, Vol. 9/5, https://doi.org/10.1002/WCC.531. [81]

Carbon Pricing Leadership Coalition (2018), *Launch of the PMR project on carbon taxation in Côte d'Ivoire*, Carbon Pricing Leadership Coalition, https://www.carbonpricingleadership.org/calendar/2018/7/12/launch-of-the-pmr-project-on-carbon-taxation-in-cte-divoire (accessed on 21 June 2024). [26]

Cardenas Monar, D. (2024), *Maximising benefits of carbon pricing through carbon revenue use: A review of international experiences*, Institute for Climate Economics, Paris, https://www.i4ce.org/en/publication/maximising-benefits-carbon-pricing-through-carbon-revenue-use-review-international-experiences-climate/ (accessed on 6 June 2024). [75]

Climate Club (2024), *An inclusive and ambitious high-level forum for industry decarbonisation*, Climate Club, https://climate-club.org/ (accessed on 19 June 2024). [50]

Climate Watch (2024), *GHG Emissions*, World Resources Institute, http://www.climatewatchdata.org (accessed on 24 June 2024). [4]

Colombian Ministry of Environment and Sustainable Development (2024), *Programa Nacional de Cupos Transables [National Tradable Quotas Program]*, Colombia Ministry of Environment and Sustainable Development, https://www.minambiente.gov.co/cambio-climatico-y-gestion-del-riesgo/programa-nacional-de-cupos-transables/ (accessed on 20 June 2024). [17]

Danish Parliament (2024), *Lovforslag Nr. L 183*, https://www.ft.dk/samling/20231/lovforslag/l183/index.htm. [60]

Dechezleprêtre, A. et al. (2022), "Fighting climate change: International attitudes toward climate policies", *OECD Economics Department Working Papers*, No. 1714, OECD Publishing, Paris, https://doi.org/10.1787/3406f29a-en. [74]

Enerdata (2024), *Chile selects the first 8 projects of its Green Tax Emissions Offsetting System*, Enerdata, https://www.enerdata.net/publications/daily-energy-news/chile-selects-first-8-projects-its-green-tax-emissions-offsetting-system.html (accessed on 21 June 2024). [24]

European Commission (2024), *Auctioning*, European Commission, https://climate.ec.europa.eu/eu-action/eu-emissions-trading-system-eu-ets/auctioning_en (accessed on 6 June 2024). [86]

European Commission (2024), *ETS2 : buildings, road transport and additional sectors*, European Commission, https://climate.ec.europa.eu/eu-action/eu-emissions-trading-system-eu-ets/ets2-buildings-road-transport-and-additional-sectors_en (accessed on 20 June 2024). [10]

European Commission (2023), *Carbon Border Adjustment Mechanism*, European Commission, https://taxation-customs.ec.europa.eu/carbon-border-adjustment-mechanism_en (accessed on 26 September 2023). [41]

European Environment Agency (2023), *Early warning assessment related to the 2025 targets for municipal waste and packaging waste: Country reports*, https://www.eea.europa.eu/publications/many-eu-member-states/early-warning-assessment-related-to (accessed on 24 June 2024). [59]

European Environment Agency (2023), *Overview of taxes on the incineration of municipal waste used in EU Member States, 2023*, https://www.eea.europa.eu/data-and-maps/figures/overview-of-taxes-on-the (accessed on 24 June 2024). [55]

Feitosa, S. (2022), *Regulamenta o Mercado Brasileiro de Redução de Emissões (MBRE) [Regulates the Brazilian Emissions Reduction Market]*. [15]

Fischer, C., B. Mao and D. Shawhan (2018), "Trade between mass- and rate-based regulatory regimes: Bad for emissions?", *Energy Economics*, Vol. 73, https://doi.org/10.1016/j.eneco.2018.04.031. [39]

Fleurence, L., M. Fetet and S. Postic (2023), *Global carbon accounts, 2023 edition*, Institute for Climate Economics, Paris, https://www.i4ce.org/wp-content/uploads/2023/11/2023-Global-Carbon-Accounts-I4CE.pdf (accessed on 6 June 2024). [85]

Garsous, G. et al. (2023), "Net effective carbon rates", *OECD Taxation Working Papers*, No. 61, OECD Publishing, Paris, https://doi.org/10.1787/279e049e-en. [2]

German Emissions Trading Authority (2017), *Zertifikate: Verkauf und Handel [Certificates: Sale and trading]*, German Emissions Trading Authority, https://www.dehst.de/DE/Nationaler-Emissionshandel/Zertifikate-Verkauf-Handel/zertifikate-verkauf-handel_node.html (accessed on 6 June 2024). [35]

German Federal Ministry for Economic Affairs and Climate Action (2022), *Auswirkungen des nationalen Brennstoffemissionshandels auf die Abfallwirtschaft [Impact of national fuel emissions trading on waste management]*, https://www.bmwk.de/Redaktion/DE/Publikationen/Industrie/studie-auswirkungen-des-nationalen-brennstoffemissionshandels-auf-die-abfallwirtschaft.html (accessed on 24 June 2024). [64]

German Federal Ministry for Economic Affairs and Climate Action (2022), *Nationaler Brennstoffemissionshandel: Ausnahmen für Kohle- und Abfall-Verbrennung entfallen [National fuel emissions trading: exemptions for coal and waste combustion are no longer applicable]*, https://www.bmwk.de/Redaktion/DE/Pressemitteilungen/2022/07/20220713-nationaler-brennstoffemissionshandel-ausnahmen-fur-kohle-und-abfall-verbrennung-entfallen.html#:~:text=Das%20Bundeskabinett%20hat%20am%2013.07.%2C%20Erdgas%2C%20Benzin%20und%20Diesel. (accessed on 24 June 2024). [65]

German Federal Office of Justice (2022), *Zweites Gesetz zur Änderung des Brennstoffemissionshandelsgesetzes [Second Act to Amend the Fuel Emissions Trading Act]*, German Federal Office of Justice, https://dip.bundestag.de/vorgang/zweites-gesetz-zur-%C3%A4nderung-des-brennstoffemissionshandelsgesetzes/290332. [63]

Government of Austria (n.d.), *Questions and Answers about the Klimabonus*, Federal Ministry Republic of Austria, https://www.klimabonus.gv.at/en/questions-and-answers/ (accessed on 6 June 2024). [88]

Government of British Columbia (2024), *British Columbia's Carbon Tax*, Government of British Columbia, https://www2.gov.bc.ca/gov/content/environment/climate-change/clean-economy/carbon-tax (accessed on 6 June 2024). [87]

Government of Hungary (2023), *Government Decree 320/2023 (VII.17.)*, https://magyarkozlony.hu/dokumentumok/37e78380d70d3d2a758ae1155c21d54e6d8d5650/megtekintes (accessed on 21 June 2024). [8]

Government of the Republic of Portugal (2022), *Novas medidas para compensar aumento dos preços da energia [New measures to offset rising energy prices]*, Government of the Republic of Portugal, https://www.portugal.gov.pt/pt/gc22/comunicacao/noticia?i=novas-medidas-para-compensar-aumento-dos-precos-da-energia (accessed on 6 June 2024). [36]

Government of the Republic of Slovenia (2023), *Decree amending the Decree on the environmental tax on air pollution caused by carbon dioxide emissions*, Government of the Republic of Slovenia, https://www.gov.si/en/news/2023-05-08-decree-amending-the-decree-on-the-environmental-tax-on-air-pollution-caused-by-carbon-dioxide-emissions/ (accessed on 6 June 2024). [37]

Heath, M. (2023), *Argentina's Massa delays fuel tax hike as election looms*, Reuters, https://www.reuters.com/world/americas/argentinas-massa-delays-fuel-tax-hike-election-looms-2023-11-01/ (accessed on 2 July 2024). [33]

ICAP (2024), *Emissions Trading Worldwide: Status Report 2024*, International Carbon Action Partnership, Berlin, https://icapcarbonaction.com/en/publications/emissions-trading-worldwide-2024-icap-status-report (accessed on 21 June 2024). [18]

ICAP (2024), *ICAP ETS Map*, ICAP, https://icapcarbonaction.com/en/ets (accessed on 10 June 2024). [19]

ICAP (2022), *Austria's national ETS enters into force*, https://icapcarbonaction.com/en/news/austrias-national-ets-enters-force (accessed on 24 June 2024). [66]

ICAP (2022), *Germany reforms national ETS to broaden scope and postpone price increase*, https://icapcarbonaction.com/en/news/germany-reforms-national-ets-broaden-scope-and-postpone-price-increase#:~:text=Germany%20reforms%20national%20ETS%20to%20broaden%20scope%20and%20postpone%20price%20increase,-Image&text=On%2016%20November%202022%2C%20ke (accessed on 24 June 2024). [67]

IEA (2023), "World energy balances (Edition 2023)", *IEA World Energy Statistics and Balances* (database), https://doi.org/10.1787/4a0c7aae-en (accessed on 8 July 2024). [3]

IEA (2022), *World Energy Statistics and Balances*. [52]

IMF (2024), "Paraguay: Second Review Under the Policy Coordination Instrument, Request for an Extension of the Policy Coordination Instrument, Modification of Targets, Inflation Band Consultation, and Request of Arrangement under the Resilience and Sustainability Facility-Press Release; Staff Report; and Statement by the Executive Director for Paraguay", *IMF Staff Country Reports*, Vol. 2024/001, https://doi.org/10.5089/9798400261237.002.A001. [27]

Immervoll, H., A. Elgouacem and A. Raj (2024), "Who pays for higher carbon prices? Mitigating climate change and adverse distributional effects", in *OECD Employment Outlook 2024*, OECD Publishing, Paris. [72]

Indian Ministry of Power (2001), *Energy Conservation Act*, https://www.indiacode.nic.in/handle/123456789/2003?sam_handle=123456789/1362 (accessed on 20 June 2024). [16]

Indonesian Ministry of Energy and Mineral Resources (2023), *Menteri ESDM Luncurkan Perdagangan Karbon Subsektor Pembangkit Listrik [Ministery of Energy and Mineral Resources Launches Carbon Trading in Power Generation Subsector*, Indonesia Ministry of Energy and Mineral Resources, https://www.esdm.go.id/id/media-center/arsip-berita/menteri-esdm-luncurkan-perdagangan-karbon-subsektor-pembangkit-listrik- (accessed on 20 June 2024). [6]

IPCC (2006), *Volume 5, Chapter 5: Incineration and Open Burning of Waste*, https://www.ipcc-nggip.iges.or.jp/public/2019rf/pdf/5_Volume5/19R_V5_5_Ch05_IOB.pdf. [56]

Israeli Parliament (2024), *Amendment Customs rates, purchase tax and mandatory payments*. [30]

Joint Economic Committee (2024), *What is a carbon border adjustment mechanism (CBAM) and what are some legislative proposals to make one?*, Joint Economic Committee, https://www.jec.senate.gov/public/index.cfm/democrats/2024/2/what-is-a-carbon-border-adjustment-mechanism-cbam-and-what-are-some-legislative-proposals-to-make-one (accessed on 21 June 2024). [44]

Klenert, D. et al. (2018), "Making carbon pricing work for citizens", *Nature Climate Change 2018 8:8*, Vol. 8, pp. 669-677, https://doi.org/10.1038/s41558-018-0201-2. [82]

Maestre-Andrés, S., S. Drews and J. van den Bergh (2019), "Perceived fairness and public acceptability of carbon pricing: a review of the literature", *Climate Policy*, Vol. 19/9, pp. 1186-1204, https://doi.org/10.1080/14693062.2019.1639490. [80]

Manuell, R. (2022), *Nigeria announces first steps towards a national cap-and-trade system*, CarbonPulse, https://carbon-pulse.com/170668/ (accessed on 21 June 2024). [23]

Marten, M. and K. van Dender (2019), "The use of revenues from carbon pricing", *OECD Taxation Working Papers*, No. 43, OECD Publishing, Paris, https://doi.org/10.1787/3cb265e4-en. [79]

Matheson, T. (2019), *Disposal is Not Free: Fiscal Instruments to Internalize the Environmental Costs of Solid Waste*, IMF. [54]

Ministry of Environmental Protection and Natural Resources of Ukraine (2024), *National emissions trading system will be launched in a pilot mode in 2025: Ruslan Strilets*, Ministry of Environmental Protection and Natural Resources of Ukraine, https://www.kmu.gov.ua/en/news/natsionalna-systema-torhivli-vykydamy-v-pilotnomu-rezhymi-zapratsiuie-u-2025-rotsi-ruslan-strilets (accessed on 20 June 2024). [12]

Mus, M., H. Mercierid and C. Chevallierid (2023), "Designing an acceptable and fair carbon tax: The role of mental accounting", *PLOS Climate*, Vol. 2/10, https://doi.org/10.1371/JOURNAL.PCLM.0000227. [84]

Norwegian Tax Agency (2024), *Avgift på forbrenning av avfall [Tax on the incineration of waste]*, https://www.skatteetaten.no/bedrift-og-organisasjon/avgifter/saravgifter/om/avfallsforbrenning/ (accessed on 24 June 2024). [58]

OECD (2024), *Inclusive Forum on Carbon Mitigation Approaches*, OECD, Paris, https://www.oecd.org/climate-change/inclusive-forum-on-carbon-mitigation-approaches/ (accessed on 19 June 2024). [49]

OECD (2023), *Effective Carbon Rates 2023: Pricing Greenhouse Gas Emissions through Taxes and Emissions Trading*, OECD Series on Carbon Pricing and Energy Taxation, OECD Publishing, Paris, https://doi.org/10.1787/b84d5b36-en. [1]

OECD (2023), *Government at a Glance*, OECD Publishing, Paris, https://doi.org/10.1787/22214399. [76]

OECD (2023), *Revenue Statistics 2023: Tax Revenue Buoyancy in OECD Countries*, OECD Publishing, Paris, https://doi.org/10.1787/9d0453d5-en. [77]

OECD (2022), *Global Plastics Outlook*, OECD Publishing, Paris, https://doi.org/10.1787/aa1edf33-en. [51]

OECD (2022), *Pricing Greenhouse Gas Emissions: Turning Climate Targets into Climate Action*, OECD Series on Carbon Pricing and Energy Taxation, OECD Publishing, Paris, https://doi.org/10.1787/e9778969-en. [40]

OECD (2021), *Effective Carbon Rates 2021 Pricing Carbon Emissions Through Taxes and Emissions Trading*, OECD Publishing, Paris, https://doi.org/10.1787/0e8e24f5-en. [47]

OECD (2020), *Environment at a Glance*, OECD Publishing, Paris, https://doi.org/10.1787/19964064. [57]

OECD (2019), *OECD Environmental Performance Review: Denmark 2019*, OECD Publishing, Paris, https://doi.org/10.1787/19900090. [61]

OECD (2019), *Waste Management and the Circular Economy in Selected OECD Countries*, OECD Publishing, Paris, https://doi.org/10.1787/9789264309395-en. [53]

OECD (forthcoming), *The Carbon Rate Gap: Consumption Carbon Rates Embodied in Trade: A proof of concept*, OECD Taxation Working Papers, OECD Publishing, Paris. [48]

Padin-Dujon, A. (2024), *Argentina removes all mention of ETS, carbon emissions, renewables from 'Omnibus Law'*, CarbonPulse, https://carbon-pulse.com/277490/ (accessed on 21 June 2024). [20]

Padin-Dujon, A. (2024), *Morocco carbon tax plans gain new momentum after EU CBAM*, CarbonPulse, https://carbon-pulse.com/257231/ (accessed on 21 June 2024). [28]

Parliament of Australia (2023), *Safeguard Mechanism (Crediting) Amendment Bill 2023*, Parliament of Australia, https://www.aph.gov.au/Parliamentary_Business/Bills_Legislation/Bills_Search_Results/Result?bId=r6957 (accessed on 24 June 2024). [5]

Parliament of Austria (2022), *Teuerungs-Entlastungspaket (2662/A) [Inflation relief package (2262/A)]*, Parlament Oesterreich, https://www.parlament.gv.at/gegenstand/XXVII/A/2662?selectedStage=100 (accessed on 6 June 2024). [34]

Philippines Congress of the Republic (2023), *An act promoting a low carbon economy, establishing for this purpose an emissions trading system and implementation mechanism to achieve national climate targets*. [21]

Promethium Carbon (n.d.), *Carbon pricing approaches in Eastern and Southern Africa*, Promethium Carbon. [25]

Republic of Türkiye (2023), *Republic of Türkiye Updated First Nationally Determined Contribution*, Republic of Türkiye. [11]

Reuters (2023), *Turkey increases fuel tax as it bolsters stretched budget*. [32]

Sheldon Whitehouse (2024), *Whitehouse and DelBene Reintroduce Carbon Border Adjustment Bill to Boost Domestic Manufacturers and Tackle Climate Change*, Sheldon Whitehouse, https://www.whitehouse.senate.gov/news/release/whitehouse-and-delbene-reintroduce-carbon-border-adjustment-bill-to-boost-domestic-manufacturers-and-tackle-climate-change/ (accessed on 21 June 2024). [45]

Simon, F. (2024), *Austria to replace national CO2 pricing scheme with EU ETS2*, CarbonPulse, https://carbon-pulse.com/287172/ (accessed on 24 June 2024). [68]

South African Revenue Service (n.d.), *Frequently Asked Questions - Carbon Tax*, South African Revenue Service, https://www.environment.gov.za/legislation/guidelines (accessed on 6 June 2024). [89]

Stefanini, S. (2024), *UK's ETS for waste risks raising costs for local govts and pushing rubbish to landfill, experts warn*, https://carbon-pulse.com/280056/#:~:text=The%20extension%20of%20the%20UK,years%2C%20experts%20said%20on%20Monday. (accessed on 24 June 2024). [69]

Stefanini, S. (2024), *UK's local govts face hefty carbon pricing bill for waste incineration*, https://carbon-pulse.com/286513/ (accessed on 24 June 2024). [70]

Surkes, S. (2021), *Israel to impose carbon tax, starting with fossil fuels | The Times of Israel*, The Times of Israel, https://www.timesofisrael.com/israel-to-impose-carbon-tax-starting-with-fossil-fuels/ (accessed on 21 June 2024). [31]

The World Bank (2024), *State and Trends of Carbon Pricing Dashboard*, The World Bank, https://carbonpricingdashboard.worldbank.org/compliance/instrument-detail (accessed on 10 June 2024). [9]

UK Treasury (2024), *Factsheet: UK Carbon Border Adjustment Mechanism*, https://www.gov.uk/government/consultations/addressing-carbon-leakage-risk-to-support-decarbonisation/outcome/factsheet-uk-carbon-border-adjustment-mechanism (accessed on 21 June 2024). [43]

Warringa, G. (2021), *Waste incineration under the EU ETS. An assessment of climate benefits*, CE Delft, https://ce.nl/wp-content/uploads/2021/10/CE_Delft_210308_Waste_Incineration_under_the_EU_ETS_FINAL.pdf (accessed on 24 June 2024). [62]

World Bank (2019), *Using Carbon Revenues*, World Bank, Washington D.C., http://www.worldbank.org (accessed on 6 June 2024). [91]

Yamano, N. and J. Guilhoto (2020), "CO2 emissions embodied in international trade and domestic final demand: Methodology and results using the OECD Inter-Country Input-Output Database", *OECD Science, Technology and Industry Working Papers*, No. 2020/11, OECD Publishing, Paris, https://doi.org/10.1787/8f2963b8-en. [46]

Zhang, Y., M. Abbas and W. Iqbal (2021), "Analyzing sentiments and attitudes toward carbon taxation in Europe, USA, South Africa, Canada and Australia", *Sustainable Production and Consumption*, Vol. 28, pp. 241-253, https://doi.org/10.1016/J.SPC.2021.04.010. [73]

Notes

[1] Slovenia's increase is the result of the reintroduction of a carbon tax, rather than a new instrument entirely.

[2] At the time of drafting the report.

[3] It should be noted there are some exceptions to this as Hungary and the Netherlands have proposed schemes that effectively cover the same emissions as the EU ETS but at a higher rate – this however would not change the coverage of emissions for this exercise and therefore a reasonable assumption

[4] At the time of drafting the report.

[5] At the time of drafting the report.

3 Taxing energy use: Developments in Effective Energy Rates (EERs)

This chapter presents the current state of taxing energy use across countries, sectors, and energy carriers through the Net Effective Energy Rates. Adding electricity taxes and subsidies to the picture, this indicator illustrates trends and considerations related to energy taxation and assesses requirements for reforms to better protect vulnerable households in an energy crisis and prepare tax systems for a growing energy demand that relies increasingly on electricity.

Although the energy crisis temporarily lowered effective rates on energy use and GHG emissions, it has also spurred the investment in clean energy that may see the global demand for fossil fuels peak before 2030 (IEA, 2023[1]). This marks a turning point for the world economy as countries prepare to step up efforts to mitigate climate change, while dealing with increasing energy demand, especially for low-emission electricity. These developments accelerate the energy sector's decarbonisation but bring about challenges such as competitiveness concerns, potential exposure of vulnerable households to higher energy prices, and tax base erosion, among other issues.

This chapter presents trends and changes in energy use taxation, focussing on their intersection with climate goals. It explores the interactions of energy taxes and carbon prices with other policy goals such as the protection of vulnerable households while decarbonising energy use, as well as interactions with other tax policy instruments such as reduced VAT rates. It further analyses the shifting of tax bases and its fiscal impacts through the rapid electrification of energy end-use with an in-depth analysis of the road transport sector. Balancing the sometimes-conflicting objectives of achieving climate goals, building public support, and respecting budgetary constraints requires foresight, good policy design, and flexible systems that allow for uncertainty related to the structural shifts brought about the climate transition.

3.1. The Effective Energy Rate and its components

3.1.1. Specific taxes on energy use require better alignment with climate goals

This chapter presents estimates on how the 79 assessed economies effectively taxed energy use in 2023.[1] Together these economies account for 83% of global energy use and 82% of combustion-related CO_2 emissions. To provide an informative and harmonised overview of countries' approach tax-based energy price signals across all forms of energy use, the OECD developed the indicator Effective Energy Rate (EER) (OECD, 2015[2]).

The world is expected to see a considerable reduction in fossil fuel use while also an increase in energy demand particularly in emerging economies with a growing population and with the continued electrification of energy production (Figure 3.1). Electricity and fuel excise taxes were originally designed to raise revenues and address distributional concerns. Today, these taxes can be important policy tools to contribute to emissions reductions as specific taxes on energy use can change the relative price of energy- and emission-intensive products and services. Governments should consider aligning energy taxation and carbon pricing instruments with climate goals, accommodate shifts from combustibles to renewable energy sources and adapt revenue raising approaches accordingly.

Figure 3.1. Back to steady growth, global energy demand overshot pre-pandemic levels in 2021 and are set to remain high in the future

Global energy supply and final energy consumption in EJ, historically by energy source and outlook, 2010-2040

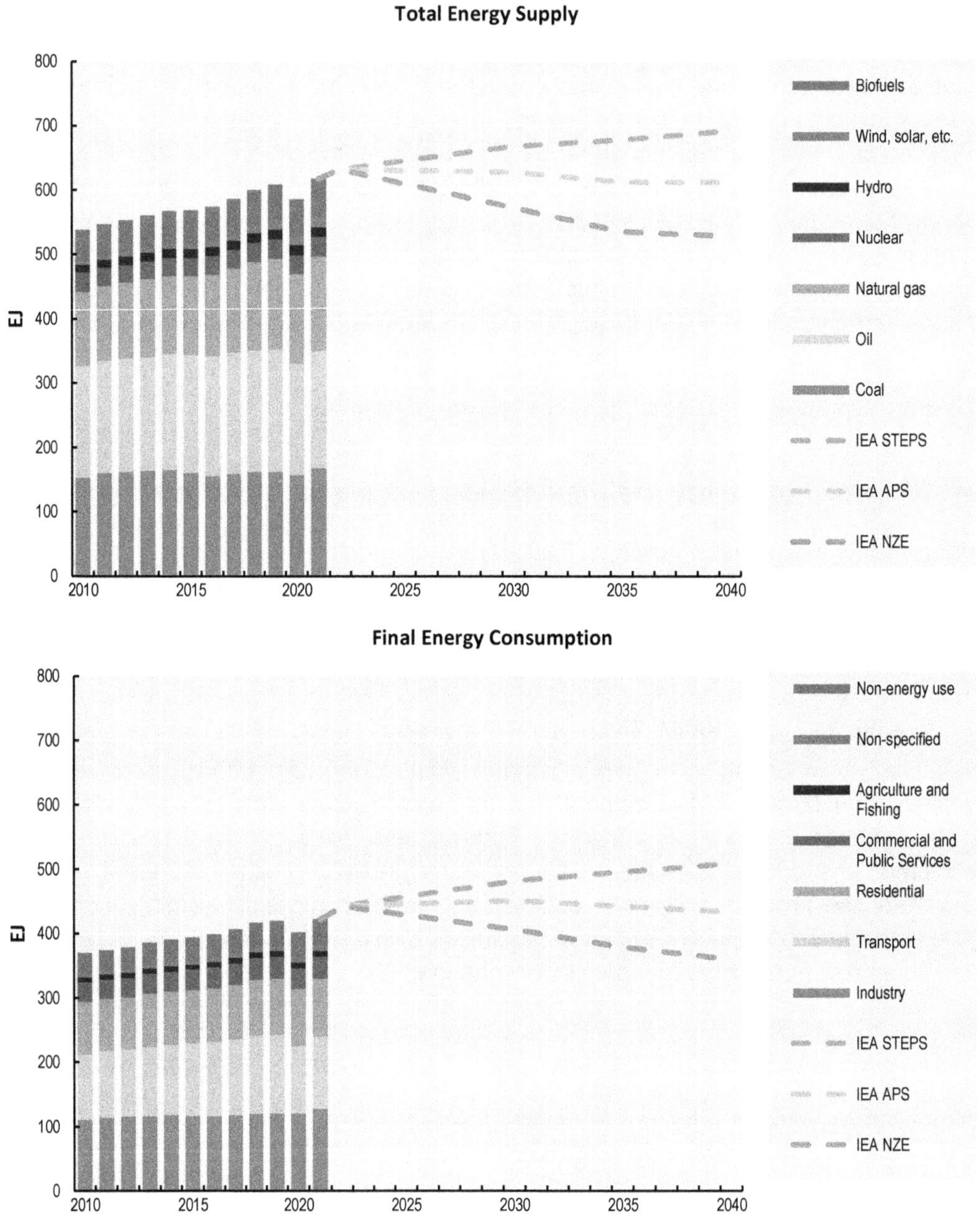

Note: The IEA models three scenarios for the global energy sector. The Stated Policies Scenario (STEPS) gives a sense of the energy system progression, based on a detailed review of the current policy landscape and provides a conservative benchmark for the future by not taking for granted that governments will achieve all announced climate ambitions. The Announced Pledges Scenario (APS) illustrates the extent to which announced ambitions and targets can deliver the emissions reductions needed to achieve net zero emissions by 2050. The Net Zero Emissions by 2050 Scenario (NZE Scenario) is a normative scenario that shows a pathway for the global energy sector to achieve net zero CO_2 emissions by 2050. (IEA, 2023[3]).
Source: (IEA, 2023[4]; IEA, 2023[5]).

3.1.2. Taxing energy use across all combustible and electricity sources

The *Effective Energy Tax Rate* is defined as the sum of specific taxes on energy use, net of applicable exemptions, rate reductions and refunds. Specific taxes on energy use include explicit carbon taxes, fuel excise taxes and electricity excise taxes.[2] The *Effective Energy Rate (EER)* includes, in addition to the specific taxes on energy use, the energy price signals that results from ETS permits. All tax rates, which are typically expressed in physical units (such as litres or kilogrammes) are converted into rates per gigajoule (GJ) of energy based on the energy content of the product they apply to (this differs to the ECR, which uses emissions as the base rather than energy). Aggregating rates and prices across different policy instruments, energy sources, end-users or jurisdictions allows the construction of a detailed picture of the state of taxing energy use.

Similar to the development of the ECR to the Net ECR, the Net Effective Energy Rate (Net EER) accounts for fossil fuel subsidies and adds electricity subsidies that change the pre-tax price of energy products and applies these to an energy base – EURs per GJ. Altogether, the Net EER captures the interaction of both positive and negative price signals on energy use, including electricity. The Net EER gives insight into how countries are tackling energy policy in conjunction with climate policy considerations and lead to better policies for economies to use to learn, assess and measure the changes occurring. The trends in coverage and the effective rates are reported, followed by analysis of several issues surrounding energy taxation today.

Figure 3.2. The Net Effective Energy Rate (Net EER) and its components

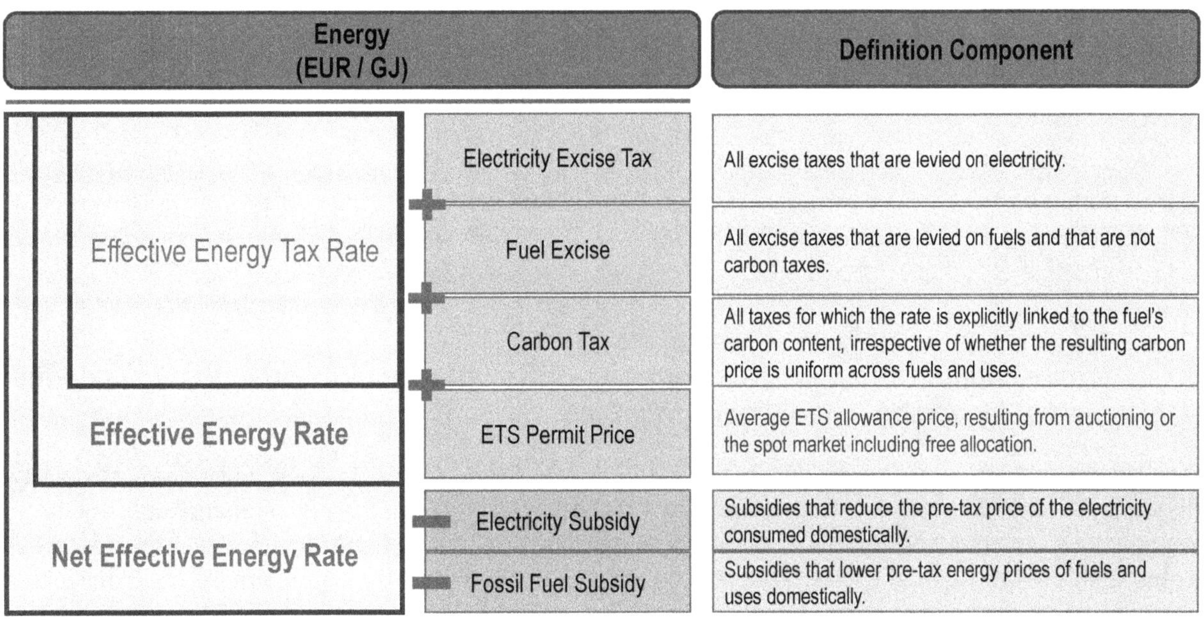

Source: Authors.

3.2. Trends in EERs and their coverage

3.2.1. A large share of energy use is not covered by a positive Effective Energy Rate

In 2023, about 53% of energy use was not subject to a tax on energy use or an explicit carbon price (Figure 3.3). High-income countries generally levy higher rates than developing and emerging economies.[3] On average, high-income countries taxed energy use at EUR 4.96/GJ in 2023, slightly down from

EUR 5.43/GJ in 2018. Covered low-upper and middle-income economies levied on average EUR 0.54/GJ in 2023. The distribution of EERs, however, is heavily skewed in both country groups. There are many reasons for differentiated taxation of different forms of energy use. Within an economy, revenue-raising, energy mix and distributional considerations frequently lead to different rates across fuels, end-use sectors, and consumer groups. Such a distribution can serve environmental goals as not all forms of energy use impose equal external costs on society and the environment.

Figure 3.3. A large share of energy use is not covered by an energy tax or carbon price

The distribution of Effective Energy Rates across energy use, 2023

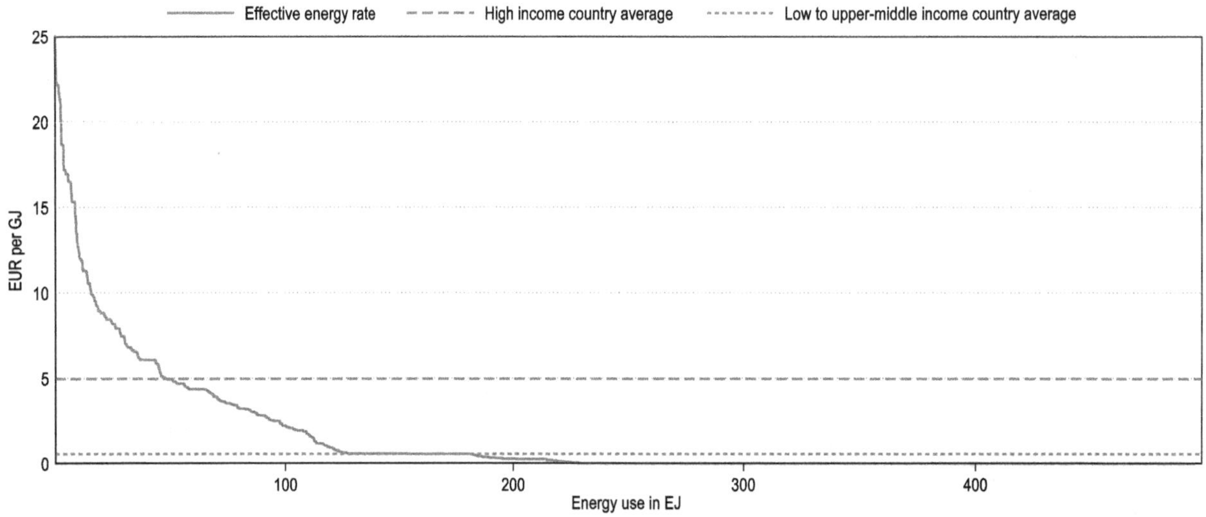

Note: Energy use data is for 2021, adapted from the IEA (2023[5]). Average tax rates do not include electricity and heating imports to avoid the double-counting of this energy use. The vertical axis is cut off at EUR 25, but the share of energy use taxed at a higher rate is negligible. All rates are expressed in real 2023 EUR using the latest available OECD exchange rate and inflation data; changes can thus be affected by inflation and exchange rate fluctuations.

StatLink https://stat.link/bdwaz4

3.2.2. Across countries, fuel excises dominate EERs but explicit carbon pricing is on the rise, in particular among high-income countries

One reason for the heavily skewed distribution in EERs is that energy tax rates vary substantially by country (Figure 3.4). Of all 79 countries covered, only four do not levy any specific taxes on energy use. In 44% of the countries covered, energy use is subject to a positive EER below EUR 2/GJ and in 23% the rate is higher than EUR 5/GJ. Fuel excise taxes are the most implemented policy instrument. All countries with a positive EER levy a fuel excise tax. On average, they account for 74.5% of countries' EER, making the fuel excise tax currently the largest contributor to the indicator. While fuel excise taxes historically accounted for the largest share in the EER of every country, in 2023, 12 countries levied a higher explicit carbon price than fuel excise tax. In four of these, an increase in their carbon pricing level (as opposed to a reduction in fuel excise tax rates) led to the change in instrument shares.

Generally, explicit carbon pricing instruments, i.e. carbon taxes and ETSs, are more common in high-income countries. Among OECD members, only Costa Rica and Türkiye have yet to implement an explicit carbon pricing instrument, although Türkiye has announced plans to introduce an ETS (Chapter 2). In low to upper middle-income economies, about a quarter had not implemented an explicit carbon price in 2023. Among these economies with an explicit carbon price are, among others, the EU member state Bulgaria, China, Indonesia, Kazakhstan, South Africa, Singapore and Argentina. Of the 79 countries covered, 58%

levy an electricity excise tax. Notably, all 27 EU member states have a positive rate in accordance with the EU Energy Tax Directive of 2003, which prescribes a minimum rate. Electricity excise taxes are in almost all countries the lowest component in the EER. A notable exception is Brazil, where electricity excises account for 91% of the EER, as well as Sweden where they contribute 33%. OECD countries tax electricity consumption on average at a rate of EUR 0.12/GJ. Only seven countries, all mid- and northern European economies, levy a rate above EUR 0.5/GJ, among them the Netherlands with the highest rate of EUR 2.21/GJ.

Figure 3.4. Across countries, fuel excises dominate EERs but explicit carbon prices are on the rise among OECD members

Average Effective Energy Rates, by country and policy instrument, 2018 and 2023

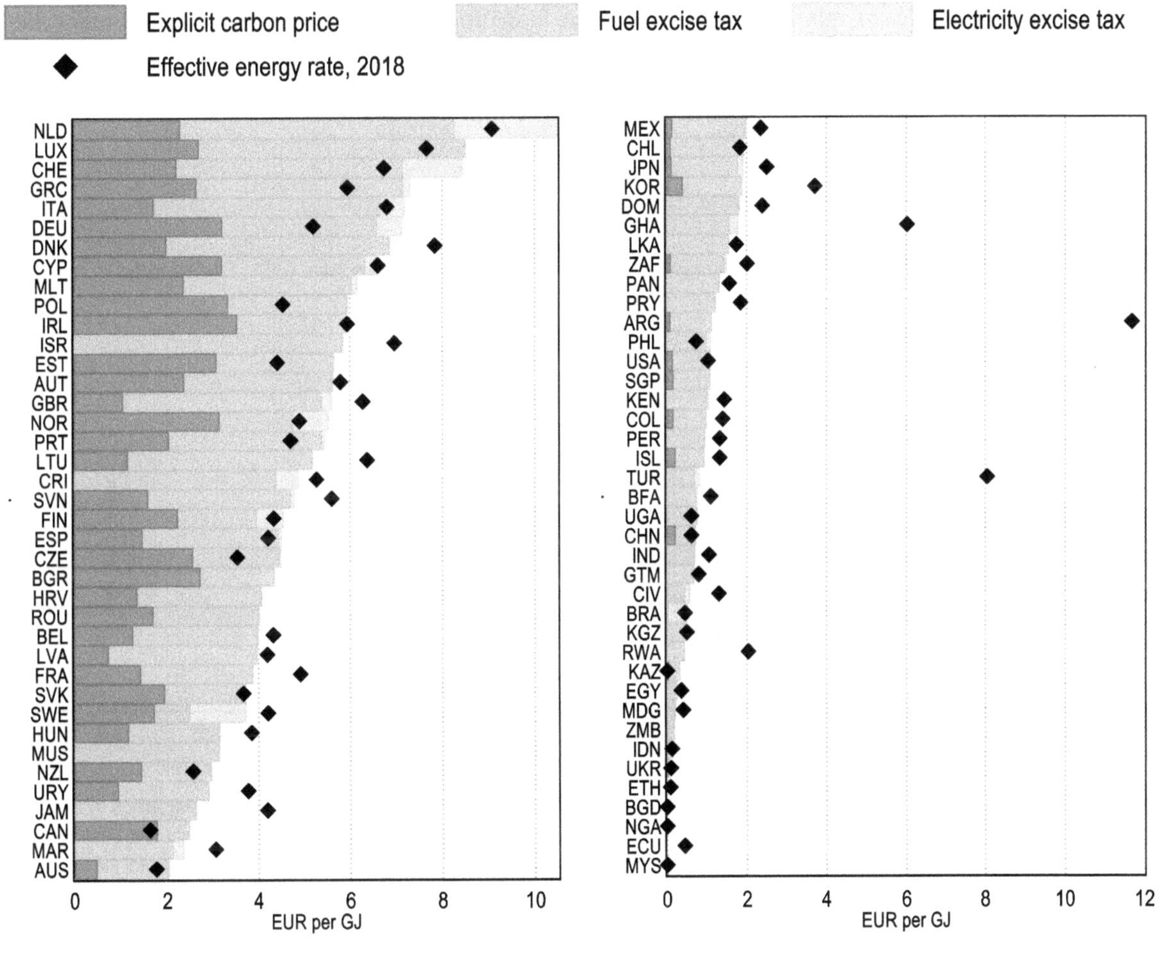

Note: While not always discernible, all EU member countries levy electricity taxes. Energy use data is for 2021, adapted from the IEA (2023[5]). Average tax rates do not include electricity and heating imports to avoid the double-counting of this energy use. All countries are covered for 2023, with varying country composition according to the coverage of previous editions in other years. All rates are expressed in real 2023 EUR using the latest available OECD exchange rate and inflation data; changes can thus be affected by inflation and exchange rate fluctuations.

StatLink https://stat.link/k509tj

3.3. Trends in Net Effective Energy Rates

This section presents the state of Net Effective Energy Rates (Net EER) across energy sources and countries. It assesses how subsidies on fossil fuels and electricity use change the Net EER and explains impacts on energy use patterns and countries' revenue generation.

3.3.1. Fossil fuels face overall higher Net EERs than other energy sources

Taxing relatively carbon-intensive forms of energy use at higher net effective rates can shift energy demand towards low-emitting energy sources. There remains scope to better align Net EERs with the carbon content of fuels and thus GHG emissions. However, incentives for reducing the demand for emissions-intensive combustible fuels are also affected by the relative tax burden of fossil fuels via other energy sources that do not generate GHG emissions when used (and are hence beyond the scope of Net EERs). Low-emission energy sources are renewable energy sources, such as hydropower, solar PV, and wind power. Therefore, a higher relative tax treatment on fossil fuels can strengthen the economic case for electrification in a reasonably decarbonised electricity mix, e.g. switching to electric vehicles in road transport or electrifying industrial processes.

Figure 3.5. On average, fossil fuels face a higher Net EER than other energy sources

Net Effective Energy Rates, by energy source, 2023

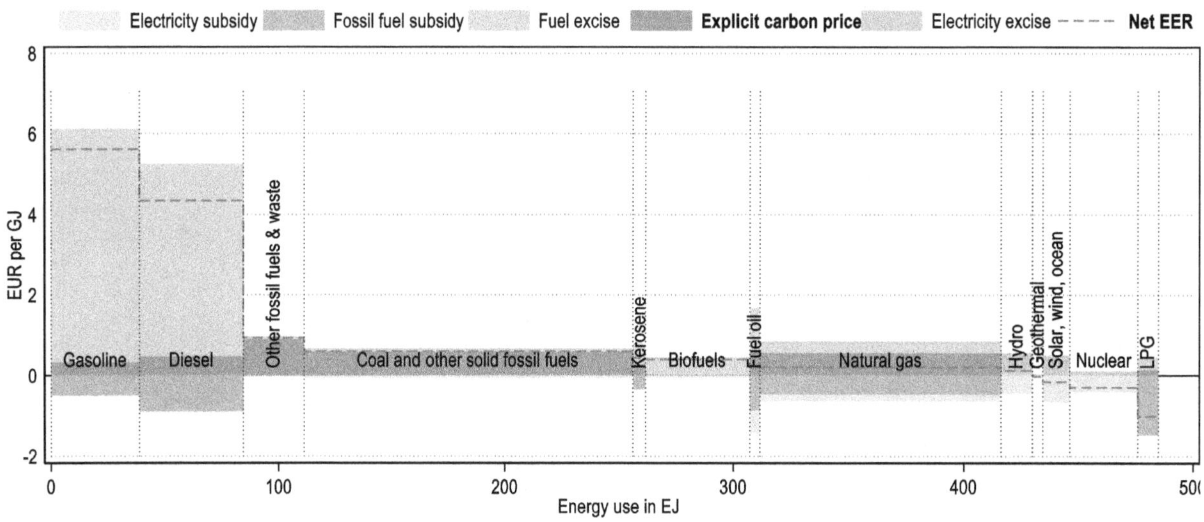

Note: Fuel excise taxes levied on hydro and solar, wind, ocean consist of electricity input taxes that were been implemented in Norway as of 01 April 2023. Energy use data is for 2021, adapted from the IEA (2023[5]). Average tax rates do not include electricity and heating imports to as the primary energy use is not known and to avoid the double-counting of this energy use. Due to data limitations, fossil fuel subsidy estimates for 2023 are based on data for 2022. All rates are expressed in real 2023 EUR using the latest available OECD exchange rate and inflation data; changes can thus be affected by inflation and exchange rate fluctuations.

StatLink https://stat.link/97y2l0

Comparing the compononents of the Net EER's energy sources shows that nearly all fossil fuels face higher rates than low-emitting energy sources (Figure 3.5). Overall, 89% of the energy use grouped by energy sources was subject to a positive Net EER in 2023, a lower share than in 2021 where principally all energy use faced a positive rate. As in 2021, petroleum products, mainly used in road transport (gasoline and diesel), faced by far the highest Net EER. On average across all covered countries, gasoline and diesel were subject to EUR 5.6/GJ and EUR 4.3/GJ, respectively. While coal, other solid fossil fuels, and natural gas faced nearly the same Net EER in 2021. The picture has changed in 2023, where coal faces a higher rate than natural gas. This change was caused by the introduction of the China ETS in July 2021, covering the country's large, coal-intensive power sector. This increased coal's explicit carbon price and thus, its Net EER, while natural gas received on average more fossil fuel subsidies. Given the higher carbon content of coal relative to gas, this is a positive development from an environmental perspective. However, the increased subsidy level for natural gas made it also relatively cheaper than biofuels. Biofuels have previously been exempted from fuel excise taxes in many countries, but more recently preferential tax treatment has been phased down or connected to environmental performance, such as higher blending ratios when used in road transport, restricting the applicable base.

The emissions-free electricity sources – geothermal, solar, wind and ocean and nuclear – are subsidised, pointing to stronger incentives for the decarbonisation of the electricity mix and electrification. In contrast, hydro power faces a low positive Net EER in 2023. This results from an electricity input tax, included in this edition under fuel excise taxes that had been temporarily implemented in Norway between 2022 and 2023. With a Net EER of EUR -1.0/GJ, LPG receives the largest subsidy per GJ. Some non-OECD economies, notably Indonesia, Egypt, Morocco, Ecuador, Malaysia and India, subsidise LPG use to provide cleaner and affordable energy to low-income households. For instance, India supports vulnerable households in the uptake of LPG as a clean, modern cooking fuel to reduce use of solid biomass. While there might not be immediate and clear benefits for the climate, such measures can greatly improve health and livelihoods through indoor air pollution reduction.

The fossil fuel surcharge – the difference between the Net EER on fossil fuels and on other energy sources (excluding biofuels) – tends to be higher in countries with a relatively higher average Net EER on fossil fuels (Figure 3.6). For instance, Switzerland, Denmark and Iceland have some of the highest average Net EERs on fossil fuels, as well as some of the highest fossil fuel surcharges. In these countries, fossil fuels are on average priced over EUR 5/GJ higher than other energy sources. However, the two indicators are not always correlated. In Greece for example, the Net EER on fossil fuels is relatively low at EUR 0.47/GJ, but this still represents a large surcharge of EUR 14.11/GJ relative to other energy sources, which are effectively subsidised.

There are 13 countries in which both fossil fuels and other energy sources are effectively subsidised, evidenced by the negative Net EER for both. While it is more desirable to send a strong price signal to reduce fossil fuel use through a positive and relatively higher Net EER applied to fossil fuels than other energy sources, a lower rate of effective subsidies can still maintain incentives to switch to lower-emitting energy sources to an extent. This is the case for Nigeria, Dominican Republic, Kazakhstan, Sri Lanka and Burkina Faso. In fact, Burkina Faso has the largest fossil fuel surcharge at EUR 16.80/GJ, although the Net EER on fossil fuels and other energy sources are negative.

In contrast, if the Net EER is relatively lower on fossil fuels than other energy sources – representing a fossil fuel discount – this distorts incentives to decarbonise and switch to other energy sources. This is the case in 11 countries. On average, the fossil fuel discount is low at EUR 1.06/GJ. Most of these countries have a negative (or otherwise very low) Net EER on fossil fuels but for some, the discount relative to other energy sources is substantial. For instance, in Ethiopia, the fossil fuel discount is EUR 3.24/GJ. These discounts can be driven by either relatively high taxes on the consumption of electricity (e.g. Brazil) or because of relatively high subsidies on fossil fuels (e.g. Ecuador), or a combination of both (e.g. Morocco). However, the fossil fuel surcharge is affected by the composition of countries' energy use and therefore must be interpreted with caution.

Figure 3.6. Most countries levy a positive fossil fuel surcharge, but sizes vary substantially

Fossil fuel surcharge (Average Net EER on fossil fuels – Average Net EER on other energy sources (excl. biofuels)) by country, 2023

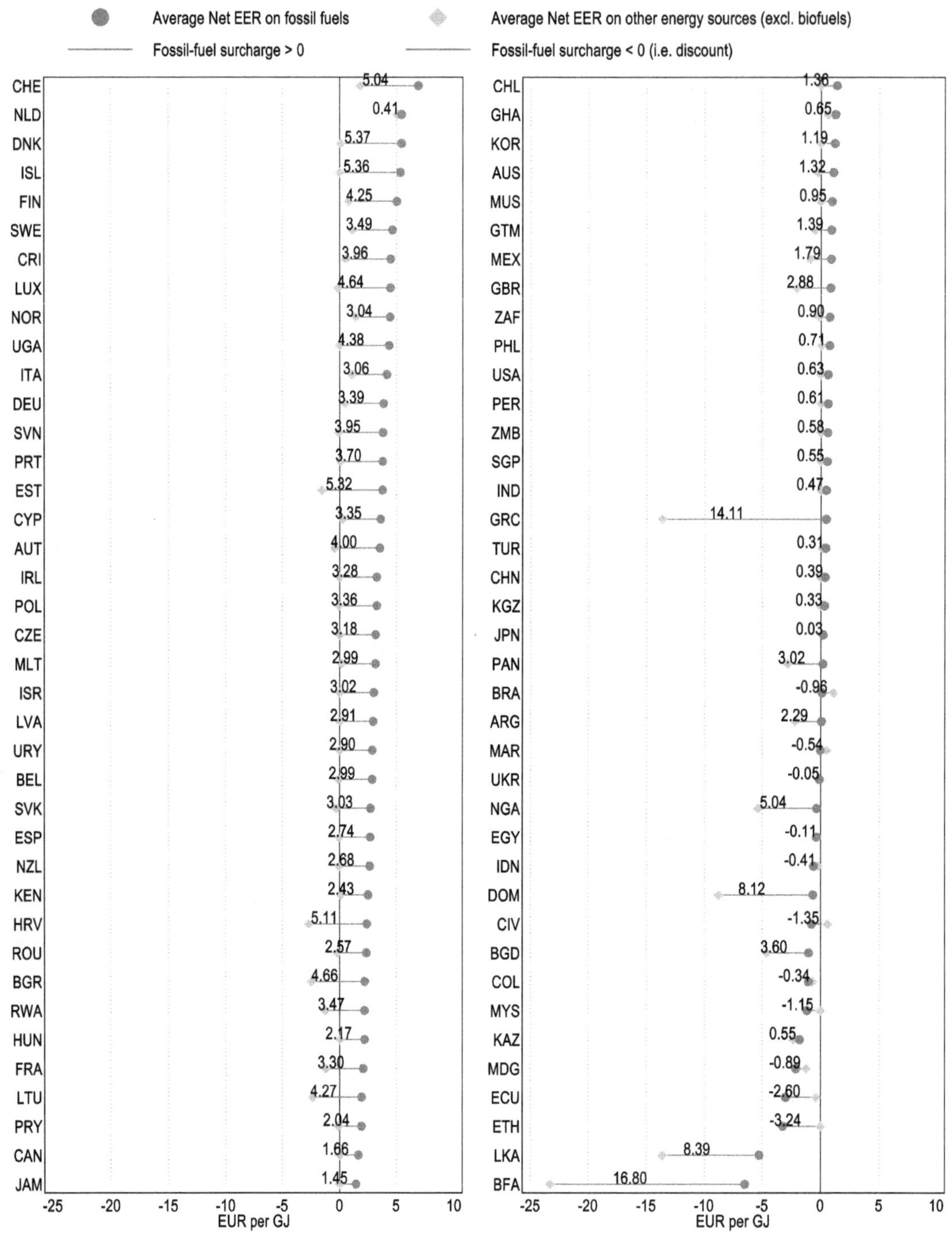

Note: Energy use data is for 2021, adapted from the IEA (2023[5]). Due to data limitations, some fossil fuel subsidy estimates in this edition are based on data for 2022. Average tax rates do not include electricity and heating imports to as the primary energy use is not known and to avoid the double-counting of this energy use. All rates are expressed in real 2023 EUR using the latest available OECD exchange rate and inflation data; changes can thus be affected by inflation and exchange rate fluctuations. Prices are rounded to the nearest eurocent.

StatLink https://stat.link/2nwi6b

3.3.2. Impact of electricity taxes and subsidies on revenues

As discussed in Chapter 2, revenues from carbon and energy pricing instruments can be a substantial source of government revenue, and the relative volume and makeup of revenues from different pricing instruments differs across countries. Overall, revenues from energy taxes and carbon prices exceeded expenditures on fossil fuels and electricity subsidies, resulting in net positive revenues (Figure 3.7). Almost all OECD countries collect positive revenues from Effective Energy Rates and net revenues amount on average to 1% of GDP, which is more than three times the relative share of other economies assessed.

The role of electricity taxes in government revenues varies substantially across countries. Of the 79 countries covered, 32 do not apply taxes on electricity use. Among those that levy an electricity excise tax, its role in revenues is still small relative to other tax instruments – on average just 0.09% of GDP. However, within specific countries, such as the Netherlands, Sweden and Finland, revenues from electricity taxes make a substantial contribution to government revenues, reaching as high as 0.6%. This is caused by a high electricity tax rate, a broad tax base due to a high degree of electrification, or a combination of both.

A similar number of countries do not subsidise electricity consumption, although there appears to be no clear correlation between countries' decisions to tax and subsidise the consumption of electricity. Among the countries that do subsidise electricity, these expenditures amount to 0.4% of GDP on average. For those that have both taxes and subsidies for electricity, expenditures tend to be larger than revenues generated. On average, expenditure on electricity subsidises as a share of GDP is 0.3 percentage points higher than the revenues earned from electricity taxes. In Burkina Faso, Bulgaria and Greece, where electricity subsidies are particularly high, the expenditure on electricity subsidies is almost 3 percentage points higher than revenues. In general, however, the role of electricity pricing instruments in net revenues for governments remains substantially smaller than that of other instruments on average.

The relative importance of electricity taxes, both as a tool to contribute to climate change mitigation as well as to raise government resources is set to increase. As economies are increasingly electrifying energy use, revenues collected from electricity taxes, as well as revenues foregone due to electricity subsidies, are likely to change. Moreover, electricity taxes and subsidies also interact with other taxes, such as explicit carbon prices and other policy concerns that include ensuring energy security and affordability (Section 3.4). In addition, an important determinant of energy-related government revenues and expenditures going forward will be how the overall tax base and the share of electricity and other energy products develop as the structure of energy sector evolves (Section 3.5).

Figure 3.7. Electricity taxes and subsidies play a minor role in net revenues from Net Effective Energy Rates

Net energy revenue estimates, by country, 2023

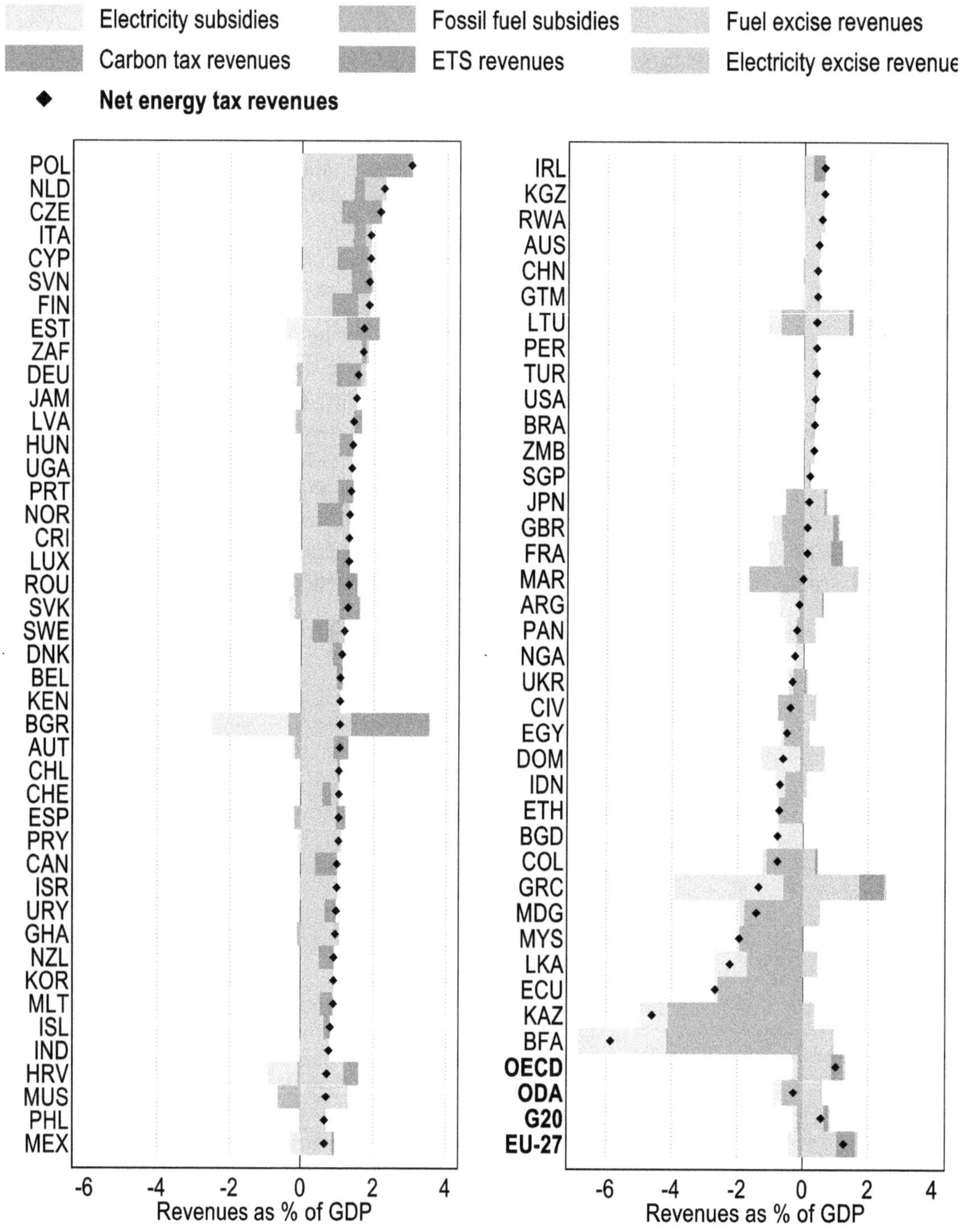

Note: Revenue estimates may be considered an upper bound of the actual revenue potential as they are estimated on historical data (fewer and more expensive low-carbon technologies, lower carbon prices, few developing countries in the sample). Estimates are for fossil fuel CO_2 emissions and do not include the revenue potential from reforming the pricing of other GHG or biofuels. Through accounting for free allocation, the net effective rates in these revenue estimates represent an *average*, rather than *marginal* Effective Energy Rate, as is used elsewhere in the report.

StatLink https://stat.link/1ae9hb

3.4. Impacts of the energy crisis on Net Effective Energy Rates

Energy consumption can represent a significant share of household expenditure, especially for low-income households (OECD, 2022[6]), and is closely tied to other policy concerns concerning energy poverty and the affordability of heating or cooling, cooking, transport and others. This dual challenge became particularly striking during the energy crisis in 2022 which had significant costs to households, and poorer households faced a disproportional burden compared to higher-income groups (Guan et al., 2023[7]; OECD, 2024[8]). This section summarises governments' broad responses to the energy crisis that resulted in a substantial increase in support to households and firms and showcases the importance of targeting such measures to support vulnerable households more efficiently.

3.4.1. Governments responses to protect households during the energy crisis decreased the Net EER of most economies

Soaring fuel and electricity prices during the energy crisis in 2022 triggered many governments to adopt large fiscal packages primarily to support households. These packages included a range of different support measures, which are detailed with examples in Table 3.1. Price support measures reduce the marginal energy prices paid by households or firms (e.g. reduced or capped energy prices or reduced fuel excise tax rates). Income support measures are split into two categories: energy-related income measures, which support income through discounting energy payments, and non-energy-related income measures, which support income through channels not related to energy use reduction in income taxes. Both can be in the form of tax measures or budgetary transfers (subsidies), and energy-related measures can also be in the form of reduced, regulation or capped average energy prices.

Table 3.1. Examples of government relief measures during the energy crisis

Category	Mechanism	Example
Energy price support	Tax measure	Specific tax: In March 2022, Belgium reduced fuel excise taxes on diesel and petrol, resulting in a decrease of 17.5 cents per litre at the pump (VRT NWS, 2022[9]). Sales tax: Spain made a series of cuts to VAT rates on energy products. For electricity, the rate was lowered from 21% to 10% in March 2022 and further to 5% in July 2022. For natural gas, the rate was lowered from 21% to 5% in October 2022 ((Enerdata, 2022[10]).
	Reduced, regulated or capped marginal energy prices	In November 2022, the Netherlands introduced a support package for energy-intensive and small and medium-sized enterprises (SMEs) which compensated SMES for 50% of their energy costs above a certain threshold price per energy sources (Central Government of Netherlands, 2022[11])
Income support (energy-related)	Tax measures	From March 2022, fuel vouchers from private-sector firms to their employees was allowed to be exempt from taxation in Italy (Italian Official Gazette, 2022[12]).
	Budgetary transfers	France provided a one-off top-up to the means-tested energy voucher in December 2022 (Borne, 2022[13]).
	Reduced, regulation or capped average energy prices	In October 2022, Poland implemented a freeze on electricity prices for 2023 for household consumption up to 2,000 kWh per year, with higher thresholds for large families, households with disabled persons and farmers (Polish Chancellery of the Prime Minister, 2022[14]).
Income support (non-energy related)	Tax measures	For a six-month period starting in September 2022, Canada doubled its existing federal goods and services tax credit to low-income households (Parliament of Canada, 2022[15]).
	Budgetary transfers	In July 2022, Germany distributed additional cash transfers to a number of existing beneficiary groups, including for instance, those receiving social assistance, unemployment benefits and basic income (German Press and Information Office, 2024[16]).
Other	Any mechanisms not classified elsewhere.	In May 2022, the UK introduced the Energy Profit Levy which imposed a surcharge of 25% (later increased to 35%) on the windfall profits made by companies in the oil and gas sector, on top of the 40% headline rate (UK Treasury, 2022[17]).

Note: The measures and examples listed are not exhaustive.
Source: Framework adapted from (Castle et al., 2023[18]).

Governments responses to the energy crisis included both significant cuts to fuel excise taxes and increases in subsidies to fossil fuels in form of budgetary transfers.[4] While some countries paused or reversed advancements of their explicit carbon pricing policies, on average across all countries, explicit carbon pricing remained overall relatively resilient to the pressures of the energy crisis. As a result, the Net EER decreased from 2021 to 2023 in most countries (Figure 3.8). On average, the Net EER dropped by about 25% (EUR 0.44/GJ) between 2021 and 2023.

While some emerging and developing economies have long-standing subsidies on electricity and fossil fuels, the energy crisis triggered in 2022 multiple OECD countries to implement such measures. In these economies, most support was initially introduced as a temporary measure for several months but has been extended in multiple times in many cases. Many measures were still in place in 2023 and a few continued operating in 2024. Therefore, the full impact of the energy crisis on taxation of energy use will only manifest in the upcoming years.

The United Kingdom and France adopted broad fiscal support packages that increased subsidies of electricity and fossil fuels in 2022 to EUR 4.74/GJ and EUR 3.17/GJ, respectively. The United Kingdom introduced in 2022 multiple income and energy price support measures of which most were extended or replaced until spring 2023 or 2024. The Energy Bill Relief Scheme (October 2022 to March 2023) and then the Energy Bills Discount Scheme (April 2023 to March 2024) provided a discount on wholesale gas and electricity prices for non-domestic consumers_(UK Government, 2023[19]; UK Government, 2023[20]). The Energy Price Guarantee capped households' annual bills of electricity and natural gas use (combined) at GBP 2500 until June 2023. Afterwards, support from the Guarantee was lowered to a cap of GBP 3000. Due to falls in energy prices, the price cap was not required until it ended in March 2024 (UK Parliament, 2024[21]). In addition, about 80% of British households benefitted from a non-refundable Council Tax Rebate of GBP 150 on their annual energy bill and a Discretionary Fund for billing authorities provided low-income individuals additional support between February 2022 and April 2023 (UK Government, 2022[22]). Further, the UK also reduced fuel excise taxes on petroleum products in March 2022 and extended the measure twice until March 2025 (UK Office for Budget Responsibility, 2024[23]).

France put in place a cap on regulated prices of natural gas and electricity, adopted sectoral subsidies for firms, lowered the electricity excise tax and introduced a one-off subsidy on gasoline and diesel consumption of EUR 0.10 to 0.30 per litre (Government of France, 2022[24]). This one-off subsidy was fully phased out in December 2022 and even with a new, transitionary measure, a voucher on road fuels, which was in place over the course of 2023- support for road transport fuels strongly decreased. In contrast, other measures such as the electricity excise tax reductions and cap on regulated prices of natural gas and electricity have been extended multiple times (Government of France, 2024[25]; Government of France, 2023[26]).

Greece took numerous steps to shield households from soaring energy prices since autumn 2021. Efforts include expanding existing measures targeting energy poverty and introducing broader measures to reduce energy prices for most consumers. As a result, the Net EER dropped to EUR - 2.77/GJ from EUR 5.79/GJ in 2021. Total subsidies in the form of budgetary transfers were estimated at EUR 5.43 billion in 2022, quadrupling in only one year (OECD, 2023[27]). Between September 2021 and March 2023, Greece strongly increased subsidies of electricity consumption for households and businesses (OECD, 2023[28]). Support was extended on a lower level throughout 2023 (Ekathimerini, 2023[29]; Ekathimerini, 2023[30]). Additional interventions during the year included tax reliefs for farmers' fuel, subsidy on heating oil price and increase of the heating benefit allowance. Responses to the energy crisis are expected to be phased out in 2024 (Government of Greece, 2023[31]).

Lithuania experienced a drop in its Net EER of EUR 3.66/GJ between 2021 and 2023. Lithuania introduced support measures for firms and households' gas and electricity bills in 2022. While electricity subsidies were ended mid-2023, support for gas was extended until end of the year and then fully phased out (Government of Lithuania, 2023[32]).

Japan introduced in January 2022 a new subsidy for wholesale energy distributers to limit retail price increases of multiple petroleum products, spending over the course of the year EUR 23.32 billion. As a result, Japan's Net EER dropped from EUR 2.37/GJ in 2021 to EUR 0.4/GJ in 2023. The initially temporary measure has been extended multiple times, most recently until December 2024 (Japanese Ministry of Economy, Trade and Industry, 2024[33]). While the support rate increased in the first extensions, it has been gradually reduced in the past months, standing in February 2024 at about JPY 20 per litre of gasoline, diesel and kerosene (Koshoji, 2024[34]).

While the energy crisis triggered the greatest changes to fossil fuel subsidies in European countries and Japan, other economies saw their spendings multiplying due to higher international fuel prices or had to expand existing measures to support consumers. For instance, in Colombia, the Fuel Price Stabilisation Fund which compensates since 2007 suppliers for discrepancies between domestic gasoline and diesel tariffs and international prices, saw its deficit rise since 2021, leading to a surge of the country's fossil fuel subsidies (OECD, 2023[27]). Ecuador, Sri Lanka and Burkina Faso saw there Net EER drop by more than EUR 3/GJ due to higher fossil fuel subsidies.

Instead of raising subsidies on energy use, a few countries also lowered rates of fuel and electricity excise taxes. Apart from Lithuania and the United Kingdom, Israel and Ireland adopted larger decreases in their fuel excise taxes to contain price increases during the energy crisis. While Ireland's response did not have any budgetary transfers, the government reduced in March 2022 the fuel excises applying to automotive diesel, petrol and marked gas oil. The measures were extended at lower levels and have been phased out in August 2024 (Irish Department of Finance, 2024[35]). Similarly, Israel substantially reduced its fuel excise tax rates on diesel, gasoline and coal in April 2022. Rate reductions for coal and gasoline were extended until the end of 2023 and fully phased out as of 2024 (Dori, 2024[36]; Israeli Ministry of Finance, 2023[37]). Denmark decreased its electricity excise tax rate in 2022 initially by DKK 0.04 to DKK 0.723/kWh and then expanded the reduction until June 2023 to the EU minimum rate of DKK 0.008/kWh (Danish Ministry of Finance, 2022[38]). Not having adopted any subsidies on energy use and slightly increased its explicit carbon prices in 2023, Denmark continues to levy one of the highest Net EERs in the database.

Figure 3.8. Governments ramped up fossil fuel and electricity subsidies during the energy crisis

Net Effective Energy Rates, by country, 2021 and 2023

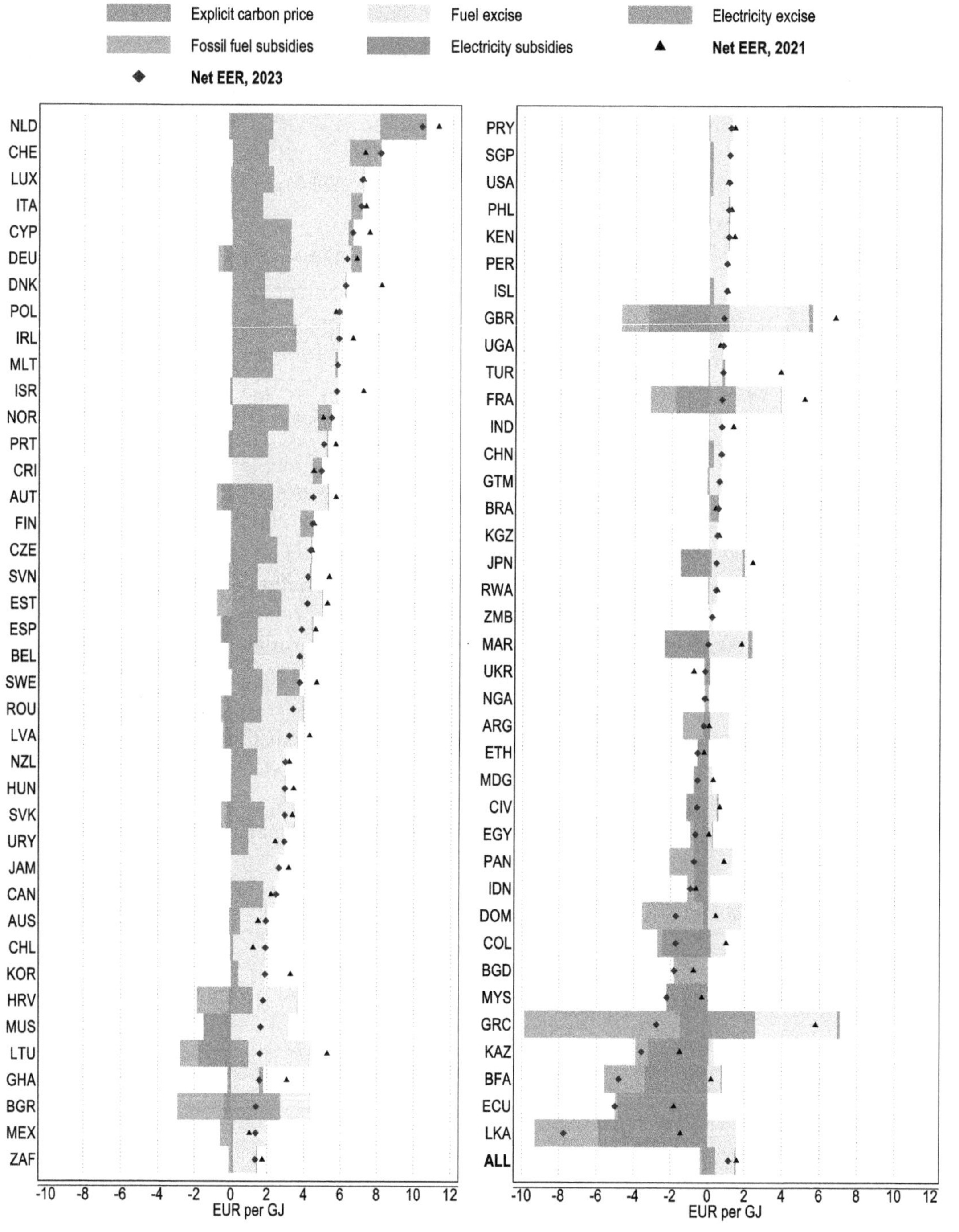

Note: Energy use data is for 2021, adapted from the IEA (2023[39]). Due to data limitations, some fossil fuel subsidy estimates in this edition are based on data for 2022. Average tax rates do not include electricity and heating imports to as the primary energy use is not known and to avoid the double-counting of this energy use. All 79 countries are covered for 2023 with varying country composition according to the coverage of previous editions in other years. All rates are expressed in real 2023 EUR using the latest available OECD exchange rate and inflation data; changes can thus be affected by inflation and exchange rate fluctuations. Prices are rounded to the nearest eurocent.

StatLink https://stat.link/ciybtk

3.4.2. Targeted response measures to the energy crisis

Some countries enacted policies that provided targeted and timely support to vulnerable households in the wake of rising fuel prices in particular for natural gas, oil and electricity (Castle et al., 2023[18]). For example, means-tested income support through cash transfers or energy bill vouchers via existing social assistance programmes, as well as other forms of transfers such as targeted energy efficiency transfers, work to reduce the burden for the most vulnerable households (Sgaravatti et al., 2021[40]). The use of existing social assistance systems allowed for measures to be introduced and received by households in a timelier manner than where new administrative structures needed to be created.

In contrast, broad-based policies such as cuts to excise tax rates or VAT rates and caps on retail prices of energy taxes effectively worked to subsidise the energy consumption of all households and not just vulnerable households. This included those that had better means to cope with the energy crisis and included non-essential expenditures such as the heating of private swimming pools, saunas, etc. Such broad-based policies tend to be more expensive for governments, less efficient in providing relief and weaken incentives for all households to reduce energy use or switch to renewable energies instead (Van Dender et al., 2022[41]). Moreover, broad-based policies can have compounding effects making their effects even larger. For example, VAT is generally applied to a tax base that includes excise duties such that a reduction in the fuel excise tax rate will also lead to a reduced amount of VAT applicable to the fuel product (Box 3.1).

With the exception of Chile, all OECD countries that operate a VAT apply one or more reduced rates to pursue various policy objectives particularly to address equity concerns for necessary commodities (such as food, education, housing, heating and electricity). To mitigate undesired social impacts of energy price surges triggered by the energy crisis since 2021 many countries introduced further reductions in VAT rates as part of broader policy packages to immediately relieve household budgets. Policymakers most commonly reduced the VAT rates applied to electricity, natural gas and heating fuels though decisions also depended on countries' relative fuel mix. In most countries, the duration of these temporary measures was initially set to about a few months, but rates were cut further and their duration extended in many countries or even made permanent. As a result, countries still apply reduced VAT rates to a number of energy products, although available evidence suggests that the application of reduced VAT rates remains a poor tool for targeting support to lower income households since rich households have a much higher aggregate benefit from a reduced VAT since they consume more in absolute terms (OECD/KIPF, 2014[42]). Reduced VAT rates that have been adopted prior to or during the energy crisis and currently apply to energy products consumed by households such as residential heating networks (Belgium, France, Greece, Hungary, Latvia, Lithuania and Luxembourg); heating fuel oil (Iceland, Luxembourg and the United Kingdom); gas for domestic use, either permanently (Belgium, Greece, Italy, Luxembourg and the United Kingdom) or temporarily (Germany and Ireland); and electricity either permanently (Belgium, Greece, Iceland, Italy, Luxembourg, Türkiye and the United Kingdom) or temporarily (Ireland, Portugal and Spain).

Box 3.1. The interaction of VAT on energy products and specific taxes on energy use

VAT is a broad-based tax on consumption, in principle applied equally to all products, and therefore does not change the relative price of carbon-intensive goods. However, in practice, many countries apply preferential (i.e. reduced) VAT rates on specific products. Through this channel, VAT interacts with Effective Energy Rates by providing a form of subsidy for certain products. Unlike other taxes examined in this report, which are calculated on a quantity of commodities (e.g. litres of fuel, tonnes of CO_2 or kilowatt electricity), VAT is levied on the sales price of the product. If the VAT base includes fuel excise duties (as they generally do), these duties contribute to the VAT burden. The VAT rate applicable to a product therefore has a dual impact on the total amount of taxes collected and on their composition.

Figure 3.9. Overall cost and VAT burden on energy used by households

Selected energy carriers, consumption weighted averages by end use

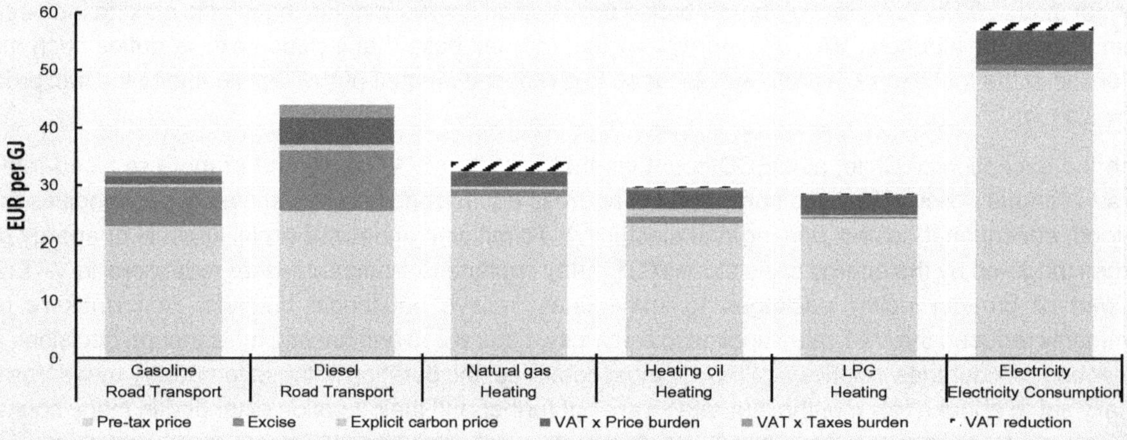

Note: While VAT reductions ('deviations from the standard rate') are sometimes illustrated as subsidies (Agnolucci et al., 2023[43]), the CPET database presents the reduction on the positive side of the y-axis for this application which is consistent with its approach on fuel excise tax exemptions and refunds. Rates and prices applicable 01/04/2023. Eight countries have reduced rates on heating fuels, with seven among them concerning natural gas. Additionally, nine countries apply reduced rates on electricity use and another seven on district heating

Source: Tax rates from CPET database. VAT standard and reduced rates from Consumption Tax Trends 2024 (OECD, forthcoming[44]). Energy use data refers to 2021 (IEA, 2023[5]; IEA, 2024[45]; IEA, 2024[46]).

StatLink https://stat.link/6in5y9

Figure 3.9 unpacks the total energy cost of selected energy carriers faced by households in 38 OECD countries into pre-tax prices, excise taxes and explicit carbon prices, and the VAT burden. Additionally, it illustrates what the total price would be if VAT reductions (acting as price subsidies) were not in place. The figure demonstrates that the pre-tax, end-use prices (in EUR/GJ) for the oil products are similar, while excise taxes dominate the tax components of gasoline and diesel in the road transport sector. The VAT x Taxes burden is only visible in the road transport sector because that is where higher Effective Energy Rates apply. The relatively lower VAT burden on gasoline is because the United States account for the majority of OECD gasoline consumption but does not apply a VAT on automotive fuels. VAT reductions have a meaningful impact on natural gas combusted by households and on electricity use. However, taxes on electricity consumption do not transmit carbon price signals. If VAT is decomposed into the VAT reduction into an economy-wide pre-tax price component and a taxes-burden component, it is straightforward to note that it will be dominated by a reduction in the former rather than the latter. In conclusion, the VAT burden or reduction is dominated by its economy-wide component.

The OECD's Energy Support Measures Tracker takes stock of and assesses the budgetary cost of government interventions in response to the energy crisis since February 2021 (Castle et al., 2023[18]). Across 41 countries assessed (all OECD members except Iceland, Hungary and Switzerland, as well as Brazil, Bulgaria, Croatia, India, Romania and South Africa), the estimated cost of announced support measures is about USD 400 billion in 2022 and USD 405 billion in 2023. Measures in the form of energy price support account for about 52% of the total cost over 2022 to 2023, followed by energy-related income (30%). Countries' relative expenditures on targeted versus untargeted measures demonstrate that certain types of policy measures, notably budgetary transfers, are better suited for addressing specific groups of the population. Only 23% of the estimated costs were spent on targeted measures, as opposed to the 77% spent on untargeted measures, meaning they benefit all households, firms or energy users the same. In most countries, the decision to use untargeted support measures were motivated by the relatively higher administrative burdens of developing and introducing targeted measures, which require various types of information on energy users. Over the course of the period, however, governments shifted to a greater use of income support measures (OECD, 2022[47]). This could reflect the relative ease with which price support measures can be administered (since they are broad-based and do not require identifying and creating channels of distribution to specific groups), or it may be an indication of lessons learned. The trend may indicate that governments changed their policy approach upon evaluating the effectiveness of the two approaches, as well public demands for more targeted measures for the most vulnerable groups of the population.

Survey data collected by the OECD (Dechezleprêtre et al., 2022[48]) during the height of the energy crisis (March 2021 - March 2022) on attitudes toward climate change policies demonstrate that households themselves also have a preference for targeted, means-tested support mechanisms to be incorporated into carbon pricing policy design, rather than broad-based support. Across all countries included in the survey, there is greater support for a carbon tax with cash transfer for the poorest households of the population, versus with cash transfers to all households (Figure 3.10). As described prior, social protection measures are one form of revenue recycling that can be used to improve the public acceptability of carbon and energy pricing policies (Chapter 2). Targeting relief measures to those who will be affected by such policies the most can help policymakers address potential opposition to the implementation of carbon and energy pricing policies.

Figure 3.10. Households prefer targeted, rather than non-targeted, support measures for carbon taxes

Support for different types of carbon taxes, in %, by country

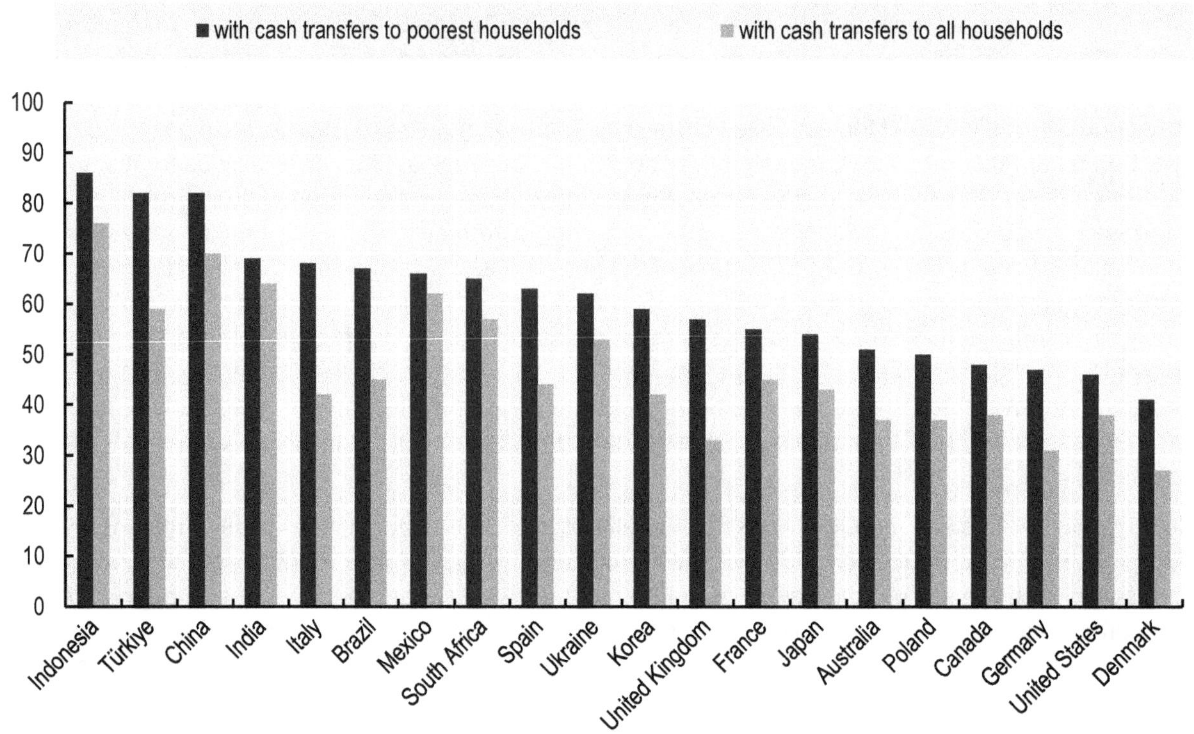

Source: (Dechezleprêtre et al., 2022[48]).

In the light of potential future energy price fluctuations, the recent energy crisis demonstrated important considerations in protecting vulnerable households as countries to move to increasing tax rates on energy and decreasing broad-based fossil fuel support measures. To this end, countries need to be able to identify vulnerable households and understand their diverse patterns of energy consumption which differ across countries (OECD, 2023[49]). Further, governments should prioritise measures that provide targeted relief to vulnerable households, rather than broad-based support in the form of fossil fuel or energy subsidies.

While fossil fuel subsidies can support low-income households, they do so in an economically inefficient way, encouraging emission-intensive energy consumption and reduces the fiscal room for alternative effective policy actions. Phasing down fossil fuel subsidies requires careful considerations to protect households from high energy prices. Steep price hikes resulting from a rapid and deep cut to fossil fuel subsidies can severely impact the socio-economic wellbeing of low-income households. Thus, the phase out of broad-based fossil fuel support to promote the transition to a low-carbon energy sector must be incremental with sufficient incentives for low-carbon investment while building robust social protection systems.

On a broader scale, the energy crisis prompted a duality of responses from governments as they sought to address the challenge of both, ensuring energy affordability and enhance energy supply security. The energy crisis promoted a surge in electricity and fossil fuel subsidies to protect households from soaring energy prices. To ensure short-term energy security of energy supply, it led to a scramble to secure fossil fuel resources, as well as investments in fossil fuel extraction and distribution infrastructure to diversify supply chains. At the same time the energy crisis re-emphasised the imperative to transition to locally-deployed, renewable energy technologies and decrease the dependence fossil fuel imports for both environmental and energy security reasons. Between 2022 and 2023, global clean energy investment increased by 17% (BloombergNEF, 2024[50]) and in 2024, global investments in clean energy reach about USD 2 trillion, twice as much as fossil fuels (IEA, 2024[51]). This sets the scene for long-term structural changes to the economy that result from shifts in the composition of global energy supply which have important implications for energy tax bases.

3.5. Transitioning tax bases from combustibles to electricity

3.5.1. Rapidly transitioning energy systems boost the share of electricity in energy end-use

Despite the turmoil the global energy crisis created in 2022 in the energy sector, it has substantially accelerated clean energy transitions, as governments have responded with stronger policies to improve energy security using low-carbon sources. About 500 GW of renewables electricity generation capacity were built worldwide in 2023. While in 2020 only one in 25 cars sold was an electric vehicle, this number surged to one in five in 2023. Heat pump sales in Europe grew by 40% in 2022, contributing to a switch from natural gas to electricity in buildings (IEA, 2023[52]). Further, the global energy crisis may be able to pave the way for phasing down of fossil fuel use: The IEA estimated that the momentum behind clean energy transitions around the world is sufficient for global oil, natural gas, and coal demand to peak before 2030 (IEA, 2023[1]). Representing two sides of the same coin, these developments bring about fuel switching in the energy demand of an unprecedented speed and scale: from combustible fossil fuels to electricity.

Box 3.2. The shift from combustible fossil fuels to electricity in the IEA Scenarios

In 2022, global final energy consumption consisted of 38% oil, 20% electricity, coal and natural gas 30%. The industry sector consumed 38%, followed by buildings (30%) and transport (26%). Figure 3.11 shows that in all IEA scenarios, the share of fossil fuels in global demand is set to decline, while electricity consumption surges. In the IEA's Stated Policies Scenario (STEPS), the share of fossil fuel consumption decreases to about 55% as electricity demand increases by 80% to nearly 160 TJ by 2050. While global fossil fuel demand remains stable until 2050, consumption trends differ by region, with strong demand reductions the United States and the European Union. In the IEA's Announced Pledges Scenario (APS), illustrating the extent to which announced 2030 climate targets and longer-term net zero or carbon neutrality pledges, changes are more pronounced. Driven by climate action in Europe and the United States and the carbon neutrality pledges of India and China, electricity consumption exceeds oil demand before 2040 and accounts for more than 40% of global final energy consumption in 2050. In absolute terms, fossil fuel use drops by nearly 45% below 2022 levels, with oil demand contributing to more than half of the reduction. In the IEA's most ambitious Net Zero Emissions by 2050 Scenario (NZE), electricity consumption would surpass oil demand before 2035, accounting for more than half of the final energy consumption (IEA, 2023[1]).

Figure 3.11. The share of electricity in energy consumption surges in a decarbonising world

Global final energy consumption by energy source and IEA scenario, 2022-2050

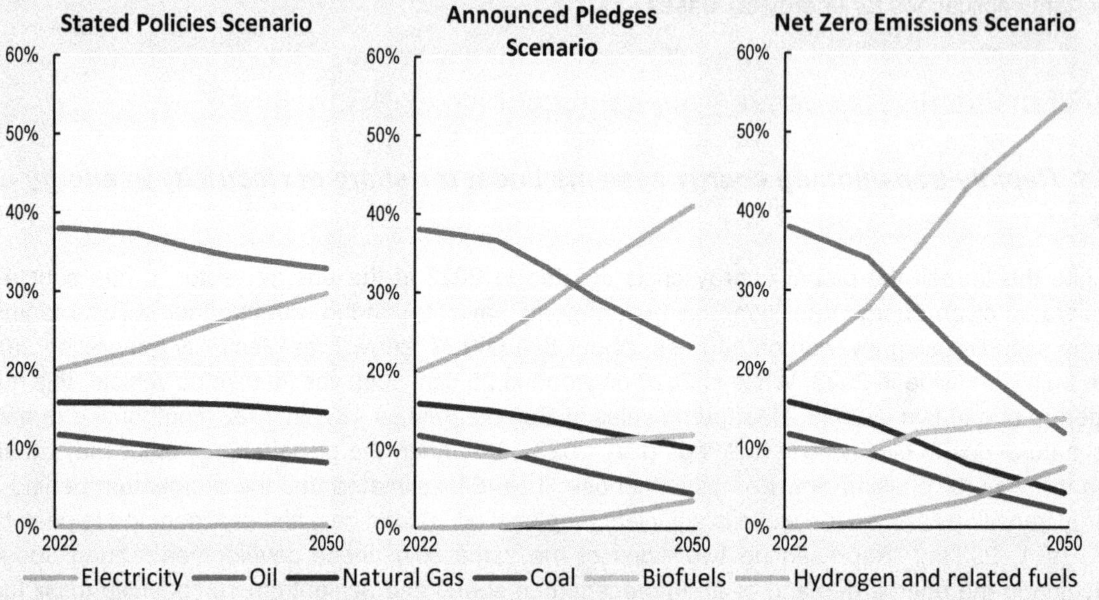

Note: The IEA models three scenarios for the global energy sector. The Stated Policies Scenario (STEPS) gives a sense of the energy system progression, based on a detailed review of the current policy landscape and provides a conservative benchmark for the future by not taking for granted that governments will achieve all announced climate ambitions. The Announced Pledges Scenario (APS) illustrates the extent to which announced ambitions and targets can deliver the emissions reductions needed to achieve net zero emissions by 2050. The Net Zero Emissions by 2050 Scenario (NZE Scenario) is a normative scenario that shows a pathway for the global energy sector to achieve net zero CO_2 emissions by 2050. (IEA, 2023[3])
Source: Based on (IEA, 2023[4]), Figure 3.4.

3.5.2. Fuel switching towards electricity requires reforms of energy taxes

Taxes on energy use are an important source of government revenue

Energy use is an important tax base for government revenues. Fuels used in road transport or electricity in residential buildings are essential commodities for most households, making their consumption relatively stable to price shocks and as a result, a reliable tax base in the medium-term.[5] Taxes on energy use accounted on average for 3.2% of fiscal revenues in OECD countries in 2021. While total revenues from energy taxes have been increasing, their average share in the total tax revenues has declined down from 5.3% in 2016 (Elgouacem et al., 2019[53]).

Fuel excise taxes on road transport fuels (gasoline and diesel) account for more than 45% of total revenues from carbon pricing and specific energy taxes. This is because, except for road transport, most of fossil fuel energy uses are either untaxed or taxed at low or reduced rates. International aviation and sea transport are not taxed. Off-road transport (including agricultural transport) is usually taxed at lower rates.

Switching consumption towards clean energy sources transitions potential tax bases

Achieving national pledges and targets to reach net zero emissions mid-century requires a strong reduction of oil, natural gas and coal consumption in nearly all major regions around the world. In the next decade, the decline is particularly pronounced in advanced economies in Europe, the United States, Japan and Korea where fossil fuel consumption has already peaked (IEA, 2023[1]). Advanced economies, in particular European countries have adopted wide-ranging measures to tax energy use and price emissions and levy the highest effective rates (Figure 3.4). Consequently, a shift away from fossil fuel use to low-carbon sources such as renewable electricity, will see a substantial decrease in public revenues from fuel excise taxes and carbon prices in the long-run. The speed of transition away from fossil fuels to electricity differs by end-use sector. It is well underway in the road transport sector where some governments already face substantial fuel excise tax revenue losses due to a declining demand of diesel and gasoline. While countries with high effective fuel excise rates are expected to face substantial tax revenue losses in the medium to long term, the transition to low-carbon energy sources such as electricity also can have positive fiscal impacts for countries that subsidise fossil fuels or are depending on imports of commodities, in particular petroleum products.

The transition away from combustibles increases electricity consumption while gradually building a new energy tax base across all end-use sectors. Examples besides the rise in electric vehicle sales are the uptake of heat pumps to replace natural gas boilers in buildings or the electrification of industrial processes. Bringing to light the importance of electricity use in industrial activities, governments in the European Union have started using reductions of levies and taxes to adjust the electricity price to steer industrial competitiveness (McWilliams et al., 2024[54]). The power sector has also begun decarbonising. Phasing down the use of coal and natural gas reduces fuel excise tax revenues but builds a potential tax base in the future: renewable electricity. As the first country in the world, Norway has adopted in 2022, electricity input taxes on renewables. The country's electricity mix consists to 98% on hydro- and wind power. An additional Excise Duty on Power (High-Price Contribution) was introduced from September 2022 to October 2023 due to high electricity prices in the energy crisis. It applied to electricity generated by hydro and wind power plants of a monthly average price above NOK 0.7/kWh. Further the Onshore Wind Power Tax of NOK 0.023/kWh generated (2024) has been introduced in July 2022 and applies to wind power plant operators subject to licensing. Generated revenues are circulated back to the municipalities that build onshore wind power to create an incentive for further deployment and act as a compensation of negative local impacts (Norwegian Tax Administration, 2024[55]).

3.5.3. Managing revenue impacts of rapid road transport electrification

In many countries, fuel excise taxes on gasoline and diesel are an important source of revenue for governments. On the other hand, the deployment of electric vehicles is well under way in major markets, boosted by subsidies and other measures. Transitioning vehicle fleets from models with an internal combustion engine to electric ones may significantly reduce revenues under current tax systems as additional revenue from electricity taxes tends to be insufficient to cover the loss. Governments need to consider how to reform their road transport related taxes to compensate revenue losses. Vehicle taxes and distance-based road user charges are important options for this (OECD and ITF, 2019[56]).

A surge in electric vehicles increases electricity use while displacing oil consumption

Over the past years, strong government support to decarbonise the road transport sector created a growing demand for electric vehicles. Many countries offered subsidies and exemptions from common vehicle taxes for electric vehicles, effectively decreasing the purchase price. Other countries allowed electric vehicles to use bus lanes and granted favourable parking conditions, making the use of these models more attractive. In addition, more stringent fuel economy standards increase fuel efficiency requirements and help electric vehicles become more attractive relative to their petroleum-fuelled counterparts with an internal combustion engine (ICE). Finally, national, and local governments consider adopting an ICE sales ban: Norway decided to phase out new ICE sales by 2025, while Israel and Singapore plan a ban for 2030. The EU and UK decided to ban ICE vehicles in 2035, while California (US) and Québec (Canada) envisage to only allow the registration of battery EVs or plug-in hybrids (ICCT, 2021[57]; European Parliament, 2023[58]).

Sales in electric models increased across all vehicle types. In 2023, nearly 14 million new electric cars were registered globally, a 35% year-on-year increase. Electric cars accounted for 18% of all cars sold, up from only 2% in 2018. However, sales are still concentrated in three major markets: China made up for nearly 60% of these sales, Europe for almost 25% and the US for 10%, while other countries such as India or Japan are still catching up. Globally, almost 50 000 electric buses were sold in 2023, about 3% of total bus sales, however, a few countries such as Belgium, Norway, Switzerland and China achieved sales shares above 50%. Also, sales of electric trucks increased 35% between 2022 and 2023. Total sales of electric trucks surpassed electric buses for the first time, with China remaining the leading market, accounting for 70% of global sales (IEA, 2024[59]).

The rapidly growing vehicle fleet consumes an increasing amount of electricity when charging. The global EV fleet consumed about 130 TWh of electricity in 2023, about 0.5% of total final electricity demand. The share of electric vehicles in electricity demand is expected to increase. The IEA estimates that electricity consumption in road transport could increase to 2200 TWh in the STEPS and to 2700 TWh in the APS by 2035, accounting for less than 10% of global electricity consumption as other energy sectors electrify as well. In the US and Europe, the share of vehicles in electricity consumption increases from about 1% to 14% by 2035 in the STEPS and 15-16% in the APS. China increases its share from 0.7% in 2023 to nearly 7% in both scenarios, but its electric vehicle fleet continues to account for the largest consumption compared to other regions (IEA, 2024[59]).

At the same time, electric vehicles also reduce the need for petroleum products. Assuming every electric vehicle sold replaces the sale of a comparable vehicle with an internal combustion engine, charging this electric vehicle with electricity also displaces the diesel or gasoline consumption of the replaced ICE vehicle, accounting for differences in fuel economy. Excluding two- and three-wheelers, the IEA estimates that the global electric vehicle fleet displaced more than 0.8 million barrels per day (mb/d) in 2023. China accounted for 45% of displaced oil demand, followed by Europe (25%) and the US (21%). Displaced oil consumption could raise to nearly 11-12 md/b by 2035 (IEA, 2024[60]).

Revenue impacts of road transport electrification – balancing between losses and potential

Road transport electrification brings about substantial tax revenue losses from fuel excise taxes and carbon prices on automotive gasoline and diesel that is not consumed due to fuel switching. In 2023, governments around the world faced revenue losses of about EUR 13 billion due to displaced oil consumption from electric cars, vans, buses and trucks. With an accelerating deployment of electric vehicles in all regions around the world, revenue losses are rapidly increasing in the next decade. Assuming no changes in rates of specific energy taxes and carbon prices, total revenue losses could amount to EUR 76 billion in 2030 and more than EUR 155 billion in 2035 (Figure 3.12). Nonetheless, in Europe, India, China and the USA, revenue losses continue to account for less than 1.0% of national government revenues in 2023. As diesel is taxed at lower rates than gasoline in most parts of the world, it accounts for about 15% of the tax revenue losses. Although China leads the global EV stock expansion, Europe incurs more than half of the revenue losses as its taxes on gasoline and diesel are about three times as high as in other regions and the uptake of electric vehicles is already well underway. By 2030, Europe faces losses of share in revenue losses of nearly EUR 35 billion, accounting for about 45% total revenue losses. However, as a share of GDP,[6] China's and India's revenue losses remain below 0.15% of GDP and Europe increases to about 0.25% of GDP in 2035.

Figure 3.12. The rapid road transport electrification brings substantial tax revenue losses

EER revenue losses through displaced oil consumption by electric vehicles by region, 2023 – 2035

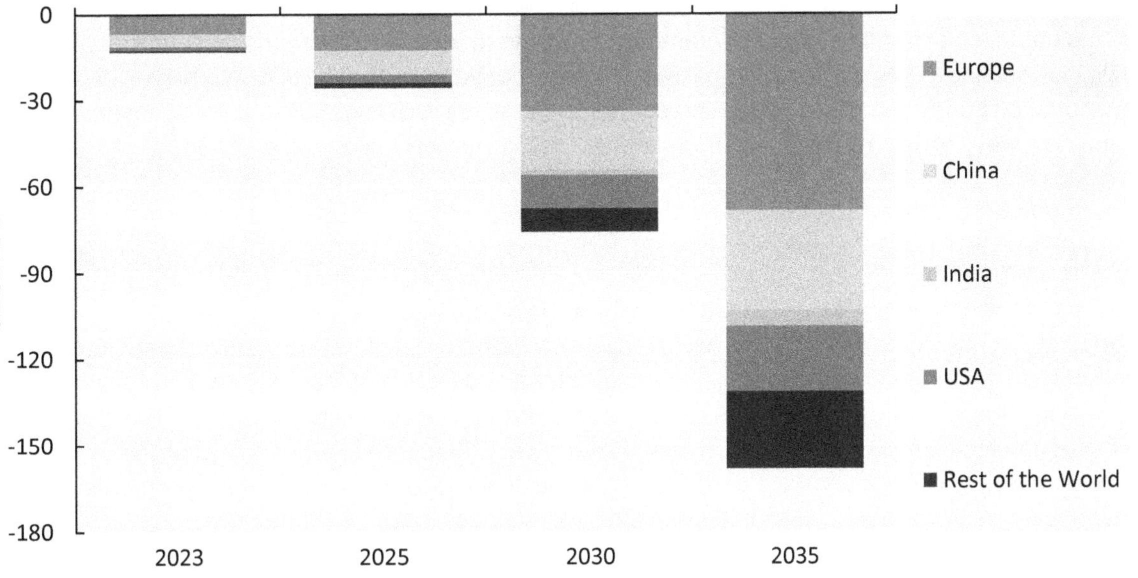

Note: Data on displaced oil consumption stems from the IEA, Global EV Outlook 2024, APS (IEA, 2024[60]). Data contains trucks, buses, vans and cars (excluding two- and three-wheelers) for Europe, China, India, the USA and the rest of the world. GDP figures are IMF (2023[61]) as a share of country-level GDP assuming 2023 levels throughout. See Section 1.3 "Methodologies for in-depth analysis" in Chapter 1 that includes a detailed description of the methodology.
Source: Authors' calculation.

StatLink https://stat.link/wxokbl

Tax revenue losses can occur both on a national level and subnational level. The CPET database has included, since 2018, US state-level taxes for road transport fuels. As a result, aggregated revenue losses from fuel excise taxes across US states amounted to EUR 1 billion in 2023 and are estimated to increase to a cumulative EUR 23 billion by 2035. Revenue losses are unevenly distributed across states, depending on the EV uptake and level of tax rates. In California (US), the frontrunner in EV deployment, revenue from the state's gasoline and diesel excise tax as well as a diesel sales tax could decrease by USD 5.71 billion annually over the next decade (LAO, 2023[62]). However, as the CPET database does not systematically track subnational tax policies across all countries, global fuel excise tax revenue losses from displaced oil consumption may be higher. For instance, in India taxes on petroleum products at the state level accounted for 3% to 12% of net revenue receipts in 2020 (IEA; Indian NITI Aayog, 2023[63]). Furthermore, the rapid electrification of two- and three-wheelers will further decrease gasoline consumption and related revenues, in particular in emerging economies such as India and Indonesia. Finally, gasoline and diesel consumption does not only decrease because of displaced oil demand from electric vehicles but also due to fuel economy improvements in vehicles with an internal combustion engine.

Electrifying road transport also has positive fiscal impacts, which cannot fully compensate petroleum-related tax revenue losses. Increased electricity consumption through the uptake of electric vehicles has generated less than EUR 1 billion through Effective Energy Rates on electricity and could increase up to EUR 8 billion in 2035. Due to relatively high carbon prices and electricity excise taxes, Europe generates about 75% of these revenues. In addition to net changes in energy tax revenues, oil-importing countries can benefit from reduced import requirements. Analysis shows that if India is to achieve its national target, a 30% sales share of electric vehicles in 2030, the country could save USD 14 billion annually on crude oil imports, about 15% of its total spending on these imports (Harikumar, Jain and Soman, 2022[64]). Furthermore, estimates show that electrifying Rwanda's entire motorcycle fleet could lead to net revenue losses from energy taxes of RWF 6 billion annually but would simultaneously save RWF 23 billion in fuel import costs (Sudmant, Kalisa and Bower, 2020[65]).

Revenues from fuel excise taxes are often used to finance road infrastructure such as road construction and maintenance or transportation programmes. Looming revenue losses are risking reducing amount and quality of services. For instance, Maryland (US) proposed cutting 8% (USD 2 billion) from its state transportation budget for 2024 amid an expected structural deficit (Brey, 2023[66]). Thus, governments need to find new ways to secure funds and fill estimated gaps from fuel tax revenue losses.

Jurisdictions have begun phasing down subsidies and preferential tax rates for electric vehicles and adopt distance-based road charges

With increased shares of electric models in total vehicle sales, governments around the world have started to adjust their policies to compensate for revenue shortfalls from fuel excise taxes on petroleum products used in road transport. Governments in countries with a substantial uptake of EVs tend to first phase out increasingly expensive purchase subsidies, then reduce beneficial tax treatment and finally start to levy new charges on the adoption and use of electric vehicles. The reform of taxes and charges often does not imply a transition in tax bases from petroleum products to electricity but a shift from energy taxes towards other pricing mechanisms such as vehicles taxes and distance-based road use charges.

Reforming the national system of taxes and charges does not only serve to mitigate revenue losses but also to increase public acceptability of the clean energy transition. As the share of EVs on the road increases, charging EV users to contribute to the maintenance of road infrastructure and upkeep of public transport increases the perception of fairness and equity within the population (Smyth and Chu, 2024[67]).

Norway has successfully scaled up EV sales over the past two decades and is today in the middle of phasing out all support. In Norway, EVs accounted for 82.4% of all vehicle sales in 2023, up from 64.5% in 2021 and expects the sales share to further increase to 95% during 2024 (Nordic EV Summit, 2024[68]). Electric car sales reached 96% in June 2023 (Marx, 2023[69]). Since 1990, Norway boosted its road transport electrification with a generous, broad policy package but with raising sales, the fiscal burden of these measures dramatically increased. As a reaction to this, Norway revoked full exemptions from charges road tolls, on ferries and free municipal parking in 2017. Between 2021 and 2023, it phased out the exemption of annual road tax fees, its purchase taxes and the value-added tax of 25% (Norwegian EV Association, 2024[70]).

China shifted its main policy instruments to promote the uptake of EVs from purchase subsidies to purchase tax exemptions in 2023, which will gradually be phased out until 2027. The countries main purchase subsidy for electric vehicles, the New Energy Vehicles 3 (NEVs) has officially ended as of 2023, leaving vehicle manufacturers without support from national subsidies for EV purchases that have facilitated market's expansion for more than a decade. China's national government had gradually scaled back purchase subsidies in the past few years before fully discontinuing them at the end of 2022 (ICCT, 2023[71]). At the same time, China extended in June 2023 its exemptions of low-carbon vehicles from the vehicle purchase tax, making preferential tax rates the key policy instrument to promote the uptake of electric vehicles. In 2024 and 2025, low-carbon vehicles sold in China benefit from a purchase tax exemption up to CNY 30 000 (about USD 4 170), afterwards the exemption is halved until 2027 (Interesse, 2023[72]; People's Republic of China Ministry of Finance, 2024[73]). About 90% of existing low-carbon vehicle models continue to benefit from reduced rates or exemptions from the purchase tax under the new technical requirements applicable in June 2024 (Global Times, 2023[74]).

The US increased overall support for electric vehicles until 2023 as the criteria established by the Inflation Reduction Act have pushed EV sales. The revised qualifications for the Clean Vehicle Tax Credit, alongside EV price cuts, meant that some popular models became eligible for credits in 2023. As of 2024, however, new guidance for the tax credits means the number of eligible models has fallen to less than 30 from about 45 (IEA, 2024[59]; US Department of the Treasury, 2023[75]). At the state level, governments start to phase out beneficial tax treatments for EVs, introduce new charges or raise fuel excise taxes to manage increasing revenue losses. About 30 US states have started imposing annual registration fees on electric vehicles, which amount in eight to more than USD 200 per year (Lee and Aton, 2023[76]). While such fees help to recover revenue losses from displaced fuel consumption, assessment found that Texas' USD 200 fee is more than twice the amount needed to replace the gas tax for an ICE vehicle. Missouri's fee is scheduled to grow 20% per year and will be three times the comparable fuel tax by 2025 (Preston, 2022[77]).

New Zealand, Israel and Iceland recently introduced a distance-based road use charge. New Zealand expanded in April 2024 its distance-based road use charges to also include electric and plug-in hybrid vehicles to compensate for fuel excise tax revenues required to finance road maintenance. Owners of light electric vehicles face charges of NZD 76 (USD 46) per 1000 km, a fee in line with equivalent diesel-powered vehicles. Plug-in hybrid owners must pay NZD 38 per 1000 km, a lower charge because they already pay tax on fuel (Smyth and Chu, 2024[67]; New Zealand Ministry of Transport, 2024[78]). Iceland introduced a new per-kilometre charge in 2024, affecting electric, plug-in hybrid, and hydrogen vehicles, in addition to revoking its exemption of electric vehicles from the value-added tax. The kilometre charge is paid monthly through the Iceland official online platform for public services (Government of Iceland, 2024[79]). Similarly, Israel approved in January 2024 a new usage tax on kilometres travelled, which will apply to EVs and plug-in hybrids as of 2026 to compensate for lost revenues from excise duty on gasoline and diesel (Ben-Gedalyahu, 2024[80]).

While reforms of electricity excise taxes do not play a dominant role, more and more jurisdictions directly implement fees on electricity consumption at public charging stations to raise revenue explicitly from drivers of electric vehicles and send price signal to moderate electricity demand from charging. In Europe, most countries levy consumption fees on public charging stations (European Commission, 2024[81]). In the US, six states have begun levying such fees in 2023 and 2024 (Glenn, 2024[82]).

Governments around the world are not just seeing changes in tax base erosion, but are beginning to experience the largest structural shifts in energy supply and use since the industrial revolution of the 18th and 19th centuries. This is primarily driven by diverse changes across the world economy to reduce, and eventually reach, net-zero emissions driven by a complex web of climate and energy policies. This report provides indicators for assessing the progress of some of these climate policies through the pricing of emissions and taxation of energy use. It illustrates with these indicators that the progress in carbon pricing has slowed with the share of emissions covered by a positive price remaining stable since 2021, modest increases in explicit carbon rates, and large reductions in overall net effective rates due to responses to the shock of the energy crisis in 2022. In energy taxation, the Net EER also decreased due to the large contribution of fuel excise tax rates in the indicator. However, the report outlines that progress is being made in preparation for the next phase of pricing emissions and energy through the introduction and development of new carbon pricing instruments – predominantly ETSs, considerations in divergent climate policy stringencies across economies, and the consequences from the electrification transition underway. Together, these indicators and developments represent a global stocktake of the current state of pricing of greenhouse gas emissions and taxation of energy use. As the world looks to 2030 targets and beyond, it is preparing for the increased stringency that will be needed to meet future climate goals – the world is gearing up to bring emissions down.

References

Agnolucci, P. et al. (2023), "Measuring Total Carbon Pricing", *The World Bank Research Observer*, https://doi.org/10.1093/wbro/lkad009. [43]

Ben-Gedalyahu, D. (2024), *Mileage tax will apply to plug-ins*, https://en.globes.co.il/en/article-mileage-tax-will-apply-to-plug-ins-1001468179 (accessed on 24 June 2024). [80]

BloombergNEF (2024), *Global Clean Energy Investment Jumps 17%, Hits $1.8 Trillion in 2023*, BloombergNEF, https://news.bloomberglaw.com/environment-and-energy/global-clean-energy-investment-hit-record-1-8-trillion-in-2023. [50]

Borne, É. (2022), *Relatif au chèque énergie pour les ménages chauffés au fioul domestique [Relating to the energy check for households heated with domestic fuel oil]*, https://www.legifrance.gouv.fr/jorf/id/JORFTEXT000046528171 (accessed on 17 June 2024). [13]

Brey, J. (2023), "Maryland Budget Cuts Spell More Trouble for Transit", *Governing*, https://www.governing.com/transportation/maryland-budget-cuts-spell-more-trouble-for-transit#:~:text=In%20Brief%3A-,Maryland%20Gov.,expansions%2C%20maintenance%20and%20transit%20service. (accessed on 24 June 2024). [66]

Castle, C. et al. (2023), "Aiming better: government support for households and firms during the energy crisis", *OECD Economic Policy Paper*, No. 32, OECD Publishing, Paris. [18]

Central Government of Netherlands (2022), *Kabinet vergoedt vanaf 1 november kosten energie-intensief mkb [The government will reimburse energy-intensive SME costs from November 1]*, Central Government of Netherlands, https://www.rijksoverheid.nl/actueel/nieuws/2022/10/14/kabinet-vergoedt-vanaf-1-november-kosten-energie-intensief-mkb (accessed on 17 June 2024). [11]

Danish Ministry of Finance (2022), *Lempelse af elafgift til minimumssats i seks måneder*, Denmark's Ministry of Finance, https://fm.dk/media/26367/faktaark_lempelse-af-elafgift-til-minimumssats-i-seks-maaneder.pdf. [38]

Dechezleprêtre, A. et al. (2022), "Fighting climate change: International attitudes toward climate policies", *OECD Economics Department Working Papers*, No. 1714, OECD Publishing, Paris, https://doi.org/10.1787/3406f29a-en. [48]

Dori, O. (2024), *Gasoline price rises sharply as gov't ends excise subsidy*, Globes, https://en.globes.co.il/en/article-gasoline-price-rises-sharply-as-govt-ends-excise-subsidy-1001466628. [36]

Ekathimerini (2023), *Gov't extends power bill subsidies for households, farmers in November*, https://www.ekathimerini.com/news/1223271/govt-extends-power-bill-subsidies-for-households-farmers-in-november/. [30]

Ekathimerini (2023), *Greece's electricity bill state subsidies for August*, https://www.ekathimerini.com/economy/1216307/greeces-electricity-bill-state-subsidies-for-august/. [29]

Elgouacem, A. et al. (2019), "The fiscal implications of the low-carbon transition", *OECD Green Growth Papers No 2020/01*, OECD Publishing, https://doi.org/10.1787/6cea13aa-en. [53]

Enerdata (2022), *Spain will cut VAT on gas from 21% to 5% starting in October 2022*, Enerdata, https://www.enerdata.net/publications/daily-energy-news/spain-will-cut-vat-gas-21-5-starting-october-2022.html (accessed on 6 June 2024). [10]

European Commission (2024), *Electric Vehicle Recharging Prices*, https://alternative-fuels-observatory.ec.europa.eu/consumer-portal/electric-vehicle-recharging-prices (accessed on 24 June 2024). [81]

European Parliament (2023), *EU ban on the sale of new petrol and diesel cars from 2035 explained*, https://www.europarl.europa.eu/topics/en/article/20221019STO44572/eu-ban-on-sale-of-new-petrol-and-diesel-cars-from-2035-explained (accessed on 24 June 2024). [58]

German Press and Information Office (2024), *Mehr Chancen und mehr Respekt [More Chances and More Respect]*, German Press and Information Office of the Federal Government, https://www.bundesregierung.de/breg-de/schwerpunkte/entlastung-fuer-deutschland/buergergeld-2125010 (accessed on 6 June 2024). [16]

Glenn, P. (2024), *The State of EV Taxation: Which States Tax, Incentivize, or Both*, EV Life, https://evlife.co/blog/which-states-tax-evs (accessed on 24 June 2024). [82]

Global Times (2023), *Over 90% of NEVs in China to continue to enjoy purchase tax breaks under new tech requirements*, https://www.globaltimes.cn/page/202312/1303411.shtml (accessed on 24 June 2024). [74]

Government of France (2024), *TPE/PME : les aides pour faire face à la hausse des prix de l'énergie*, https://www.economie.gouv.fr/entreprises/tpe-pme-aides-hausse-prix-energie. [25]

Government of France (2023), *Programme de Stabilité*, Government of France. [26]

Government of France (2022), *Décret n° 2022-423 du 25 mars 2022 relatif à l'aide exceptionnelle à l'acquisition de carburants*, https://www.legifrance.gouv.fr/jorf/id/JORFTEXT000045410518. [24]

Government of Greece (2023), *Draft Budgetary Plan 2024*, https://economy-finance.ec.europa.eu/system/files/2023-10/2024_dbp_el_en.pdf. [31]

Government of Iceland (2024), *Kilometer fee for electric, hydrogen and plug-in hybrid cars*, https://island.is/en/kilometer-fee (accessed on 24 June 2024). [79]

Government of Lithuania (2023), *2024 Lithuanian Draft Budgetary Plan*, https://finmin.lrv.lt/media/viesa/saugykla/2024/1/dPHsAFBCFvE.pdf. [32]

Guan, Y. et al. (2023), "Burden of the global energy price crisis on households", *Nature Energy 2023 8:3*, Vol. 8/3, pp. 304-316, https://doi.org/10.1038/s41560-023-01209-8. [7]

Harikumar, A., H. Jain and A. Soman (2022), *India's Electric Vehicle Transition: Managing Fuel Tax Revenue Loss*, CEEW, https://www.ceew.in/sites/default/files/ceew-research-on-recovering-fuel-tax-revenue-loss-from-ev-transition-in-india.pdf (accessed on 24 June 2024). [64]

ICCT (2023), *Accelerating new energy vehicle uptake in Chinese cities: A 2023 policy update in a post-subsidy era*, International Council on Clean Transportation, https://theicct.org/publication/accelerating-new-energy-vehicle-uptake-in-chinese-cities-2023-policy-update-post-subsidy-era-dec23/ (accessed on 24 June 2024). [71]

ICCT (2021), *Fact Sheet 05. Regulatory design elements: Phase-out targets for combustion engine vehicles*, International Council on Clean Transportation, https://theicct.org/wp-content/uploads/2021/12/eu-co2-FS5-jun2021.pdf (accessed on 24 June 2024). [57]

IEA (2024), "End-use prices: Energy prices in national currency per toe", *IEA Energy Prices and Taxes Statistics* (database), https://doi.org/10.1787/data-00440-en (accessed on 10 May 2024). [46]

IEA (2024), *Global EV Outlook 2024*, https://www.iea.org/reports/global-ev-outlook-2024. [59]

IEA (2024), *Global EV Outlook 2024 Data (database)*, International Energy Agency, Paris, https://www.iea.org/reports/global-ev-outlook-2024 (accessed on 24 June 2024). [60]

IEA (2024), "Transport sector detailed data and indicators", *IEA Energy Efficiency Indicators* (database), https://doi.org/10.1787/57cc7c07-en (accessed on 10 May 2024). [45]

IEA (2024), *World Energy Investment 2024*, IEA, https://www.iea.org/reports/world-energy-investment-2024. [51]

IEA (2023), *Global Energy and Climate Model*, IEA, https://www.iea.org/reports/global-energy-and-climate-model. [3]

IEA (2023), *Global heat pump sales continue double-digit growth*, International Energy Agency, https://www.iea.org/commentaries/global-heat-pump-sales-continue-double-digit-growth (accessed on 24 June 2024). [52]

IEA (2023), *Terms and Conditions*, http://www.iea.org/terms (accessed on 6 June 2024). [1]

IEA (2023), "World energy balances (Edition 2023)", *IEA World Energy Statistics and Balances* (database), https://doi.org/10.1787/4a0c7aae-en (accessed on 8 July 2024). [39]

IEA (2023), *World Energy Outlook 2023*, https://www.iea.org/reports/world-energy-outlook-2023 (accessed on 6 June 2024). [4]

IEA (2023), *World Energy Statistics and Balances*, https://www.oecd-ilibrary.org/energy/data/iea-world-energy-statistics-and-balances/world-energy-balances-edition-2023_4a0c7aae-en (accessed on 10 June 2024). [5]

IEA; Indian NITI Aayog (2023), *Transitioning India's Road Transport Sector*, https://www.iea.org/reports/transitioning-indias-road-transport-sector. [63]

Interesse, G. (2023), *China Extends NEV Tax Reduction and Exemption Policy to 2027*, China Briefing, https://www.china-briefing.com/news/china-extends-nev-tax-reduction-and-exemption-policy-to-2027/ (accessed on 24 June 2024). [72]

International Monetary Fund (2023), *World Economic Outlook 2023: Navigating Global Divergences*. [61]

Irish Department of Finance (2024), *Budget 2024: Tax Policy Changes*, Ireland's Department of Finance, https://www.gov.ie/en/publication/de3d4-budget-2024-taxation-measures/. [35]

Israeli Ministry of Finance (2023), *Signed decrees to extend the effectuality of the tax reduction on coal*, https://www.gov.il/en/pages/press_23012023. [37]

Italian Official Gazette (2022), *Misure urgenti per contrastare gli effetti economici e umanitari della crisi ucraina [Urgent measures to counter the economic and humanitarian effects of the Ukrainian crisis]*, https://www.gazzettaufficiale.it/eli/id/2022/03/21/22G00032/SG (accessed on 17 June 2024). [12]

Japanese Ministry of Economy, Trade and Industry (2024), *Press Conference by Minister Saito (Excerpt)*, https://www.meti.go.jp/english/speeches/press_conferences/2024/0628001.html. [33]

Koshoji, H. (2024), *Japan cuts fuel subsidy for Feb 15-21 on weak crude oil prices*, S&P Global, https://www.spglobal.com/commodityinsights/en/market-insights/latest-news/oil/021524-japan-cuts-fuel-subsidy-for-feb-15-21-on-weak-crude-oil-prices. [34]

LAO (2023), *Assessing California's Climate Policies—Implications for State Transportation Funding and Programs*, California Legislative Analysist's Office, https://lao.ca.gov/Publications/Report/4821 (accessed on 24 June 2024). [62]

Lee, M. and A. Aton (2023), *Electric cars face 'punitive' fees, new restrictions in many states*, Politico, https://www.politico.com/news/2023/08/17/punitive-texas-other-states-roadblocks-ev-transition-00110125 (accessed on 24 June 2024). [76]

Marx, W. (2023), *Norway Struggles to Pull the Plug on EV Subsidies*, https://www.bloomberg.com/news/articles/2023-07-26/norway-pulls-the-plug-on-ev-tax-incentives-and-subsidies (accessed on 24 June 2024). [69]

McWilliams, B. et al. (2024), *Europe's under-the-radar industrial policy: intervention in electricity pricing*, https://www.bruegel.org/policy-brief/europes-under-radar-industrial-policy-intervention-electricity-pricing (accessed on 24 June 2024). [54]

New Zealand Ministry of Transport (2024), *Road User Charges system*, https://www.transport.govt.nz/area-of-interest/revenue/road-user-charges-system#:~:text=RUC%20is%20a%20distance%20charging,some%20trailers%2C%20must%20pay%20RUC. (accessed on 24 June 2024). [78]

Nordic EV Summit (2024), *4 out of 5 new cars in Norway are now fully electric*, https://nordicevs.no/evs-continue-to-dominate-norwegian-car-sales-in-2023-4-out-of-5-new-cars-now-fully-electric/#:~:text=NEARLY%20100%25%20ELECTRIC%3A%20Fast%20charging,car%20sales%20in%20the%20market. (accessed on 24 June 2024). [68]

Norwegian EV Association (2024), *Norwegian EV Policy*, https://elbil.no/english/norwegian-ev-policy/ (accessed on 24 June 2024). [70]

Norwegian Tax Administration (2024), *Excise duty on onshore wind energy*, https://www.skatteetaten.no/en/business-and-organisation/vat-and-duties/excise-duties/about-the-excise-duties/excise-duty-on-onshore-wind-energy/. [55]

OECD (2024), *OECD Employment Outlook 2024*, OECD, Paris, https://www.oecd.org/en/publications/oecd-employment-outlook-2024_ac8b3538-en.html. [8]

OECD (2023), *How Green is Household Behaviour?: Sustainable Choices in a Time of Interlocking Crises*, OECD Studies on Environmental Policy and Household Behaviour, OECD Publishing, Paris, https://doi.org/10.1787/2bbbb663-en. [49]

OECD (2023), *OECD Economic Surveys: Greece 2023*, OECD, Paris, https://www.oecd-ilibrary.org/economics/oecd-economic-surveys-greece-2023_c5f11cd5-en. [28]

OECD (2023), *OECD Inventory of Support Measures for Fossil Fuels 2023*, OECD Publishing, Paris, https://doi.org/10.1787/87dc4a55-en. [27]

OECD (2022), *OECD Economic Outlook, Volume 2022 Issue 2*, OECD Publishing, Paris, https://doi.org/10.1787/f6da2159-en. [6]

OECD (2022), *Tax Policy Reforms 2022: OECD and Selected Partner Economies*, OECD Publishing, Paris, https://doi.org/10.1787/067c593d-en. [47]

OECD (2015), *Taxing Energy Use 2015: OECD and Selected Partner Economies*, OECD Publishing, Paris, https://doi.org/10.1787/9789264232334-en. [2]

OECD (forthcoming), *Consumption Tax Trends 2024: VAT/GST and Excise Rates, Trends and Policy Issues*, OECD Publishing, Paris. [44]

OECD/KIPF (2014), *The Distributional Effects of Consumption Taxes in OECD Countries*, OECD Tax Policy Studies, No. 22, OECD Publishing, Paris, https://doi.org/10.1787/9789264224520-en. [42]

OECD and ITF (2019), *Tax Revenue Implications of Decarbonising Road Transport: Scenarios for Slovenia*, OECD Publishing, Paris, https://doi.org/10.1787/87b39a2f-en. [56]

Parliament of Canada (2022), *An Act to amend the Income Tax Act (temporary enhancement to the Goods and Services Tax/Harmonized Sales Tax credit)*, https://www.parl.ca/legisinfo/en/bill/44-1/c-30 (accessed on 17 June 2024). [15]

People's Republic of China Ministry of Finance (2024), *Announcement No. 10 of 2023 of the Ministry of Finance (Announcement on the extension and optimization of the vehicle purchase tax exemption policy for new energy vehicles)*, People's Republic of China Ministry of Finance. [73]

Polish Chancellery of the Prime Minister (2022), *We have frozen costs of electricity for Poles for 2023.*, Website of the Republic of Poland, https://www.gov.pl/web/primeminister/We-have-frozen-costs-of-electricity-for-Poles-for-2023 (accessed on 17 June 2024). [14]

Preston, B. (2022), *High Registration Fees Hamper Adoption of Electric Vehicles*, https://www.consumerreports.org/cars/hybrids-evs/high-registration-fees-hamper-adoption-of-electric-vehicles-a2396438631/ (accessed on 24 June 2024). [77]

Sgaravatti, G. et al. (2021), *National fiscal policy responses to the energy crisis*, Bruegel Datasets, https://www.bruegel.org/dataset/national-policies-shield-consumers-rising-energy-prices (accessed on 6 June 2024). [40]

Smyth, J. and A. Chu (2024), "Governments slap taxes on EVs as $110bn fuel duty shortfall looms", *Financial Times*, https://www.ft.com/content/9e4e38af-acb6-426b-9cd5-5f7e938d4443. [67]

Sudmant, A., E. Kalisa and J. Bower (2020), *The impact of scaling up electric motorbikes in Rwanda*, International Growth Center, https://www.theigc.org/sites/default/files/2020/08/Sudmant-et-al-2020-policy-brief_v2.pdf (accessed on 24 June 2024). [65]

UK Government (2023), *Energy Bill Relief Scheme: help for businesses and other non-domestic customers*, https://www.gov.uk/guidance/energy-bill-relief-scheme-help-for-businesses-and-other-non-domestic-customers. [20]

UK Government (2023), *Energy Bills Discount Scheme*, https://www.gov.uk/guidance/energy-bills-discount-scheme. [19]

UK Government (2022), *Support for energy bills - the council tax rebate 2022-23: billing authority guidance*, https://www.gov.uk/government/publications/the-council-tax-rebate-2022-23-billing-authority-guidance/support-for-energy-bills-the-council-tax-rebate-2022-23-billing-authority-guidance. [22]

UK Office for Budget Responsibility (2024), *Economic and Fiscal Outlook*, https://obr.uk/efo/economic-and-fiscal-outlook-march-2024/. [23]

UK Parliament (2024), *Gas and electricity prices during the 'energy crisis' and beyond*, https://commonslibrary.parliament.uk/research-briefings/cbp-9714/. [21]

UK Treasury (2022), *Energy Profits Levy Factsheet*, https://www.gov.uk/government/publications/cost-of-living-support/energy-profits-levy-factsheet-26-may-2022 (accessed on 6 June 2024). [17]

US Department of the Treasury (2023), *Treasury Releases Proposed Guidance to Continue U.S. Manufacturing Boom in Batteries and Clean Vehicles, Strengthen Energy Security*, https://home.treasury.gov/news/press-releases/jy1939 (accessed on 24 June 2024). [75]

Van Dender, K. et al. (2022), "Why governments should target support amidst high energy prices", *Policy Responses: Ukraine*, OECD Publishing , Paris, https://www.iea.org/reports/oil- (accessed on 6 June 2024). [41]

VRT NWS (2022), *Big fall in the price of petrol and diesel*, VRT NWS, https://www.vrt.be/vrtnws/en/2022/03/18/big-fall-in-the-price-of-petrol-and-diesel/ (accessed on 6 June 2024). [9]

Notes

[1] The tax rates for this edition reflect rates applicable on 1 April 2023, while ETS permit price reflect changes over the course of 2023.

[2] Electricity can be subject to multiple different taxes, charges and fees. The CPET database only models electricity excise taxes as these consistently apply to electricity use on pre-tax, end-use prices. Other charges and fees are not necessarily applied to pre-tax, end-use prices but are fixed costs associated with the provision of electricity. Further, many fixed costs associated with the provision of electricity, e.g. for network infrastructure, are recuperated at the margin (though network tariffs that are charged on a volumetric basis).

[3] The division is based on the World Bank's country classification (Table A.3. World Bank Country Classification). High-income economies are those with a GNI per capita of USD 13 846 or more in 2022.

[4] While reductions in fuel excise tax rates are effectively subsidising the use of a specific fuel (e.g. gasoline or diesel), they are reflected in the Net EER as lowering rates of fuel excise taxes. In contrast, fossil fuel subsidies in form of budgetary transfers feed into the Net ECR as a negative price component.

[5] Energy products have a relatively low own price elasticity of demand. The own price-elasticity is measured by the extent to which a percentage increase in the price of a good leads to percentage decrease in the demand for it.

[6] GDP projections used in this analysis follow assumption of the IEA Global EV Outlook 2024 (IEA, 2024[60]).

Annex A. Country and energy definitions

Table A.1 Energy product definitions

Product classification	Product category	Product definition	Included in GHG emissions dataset (Chapter 2)?	Included in energy content dataset (Chapter 3)?
Fossil fuels:	Coal and other solid fossil fuels	Anthracite; bitumen; bituminous coal; brown coal briquettes; coke oven coke; coking coal; gas coke; lignite; oil shale; patent fuel; peat; peat products; petroleum coke; sub-bituminous coal	Yes	Yes
	Fuel oil	Fuel oil	Yes	Yes
	Diesel	Gas/diesel oil excl. biofuels	Yes	Yes
	Kerosene	Jet kerosene; other kerosene	Yes	Yes
	Gasoline	Aviation gasoline; jet gasoline; motor gasoline excl. biofuels	Yes	Yes
	LPG	Liquefied petroleum gas	Yes	Yes
	Natural gas	Natural gas	Yes	Yes
	Other fossil fuels and non-renewable waste	Additives; blast furnace gas; coal tar; coke oven gas; converter gas; crude oil; ethane; gas works gas; industrial waste lubricants; municipal waste (non-renewable); naphtha; natural gas liquids; other hydrocarbons; other oil products; paraffin waxes; refinery feedstocks; refinery gas; white and industrial spirit	Yes	Yes
Biofuels:	Biofuels	Biodiesels; biogases; biogasoline; bio jet kerosene; charcoal; municipal waste (renewable); other liquid biofuels; primary solid biofuels	CO2 emissions from the combustion of biofuels included as memo item only.	Yes
Non-combustible energy sources:	Hydro	Hydro	No	Yes
	Geothermal	Geothermal	No	Yes
	Solar, wind, ocean	Solar photovoltaics; solar thermal; tide, wave and ocean; wind	No	Yes
	Nuclear	Nuclear	No	Yes
	Other electricity and heating sources	Electricity imports; heating imports; other elec. & heat. sources	No	Yes

Note: Own classification. Energy products are as defined in the IEA's World Energy Statistics and Balances.

Table A.2. CPET database country coverage

Geographic coverage for years used in the report. Countries are ordered alphabetically in terms of their ISO codes.

Country	ISO alpha-3 code	2018	2021	2023
Argentina	ARG	Yes	Yes	Yes
Australia	AUS	Yes	Yes	Yes
Austria	AUT	Yes	Yes	Yes
Belgium	BEL	Yes	Yes	Yes
Burkina Faso	BFA	Yes	Yes	Yes
Bangladesh	BGD	Yes	Yes	Yes
Bulgaria	BGR			Yes
Brazil	BRA	Yes	Yes	Yes
Canada	CAN	Yes	Yes	Yes
Switzerland	CHE	Yes	Yes	Yes
Chile	CHL	Yes	Yes	Yes
China	CHN	Yes	Yes	Yes
Côte d'Ivoire	CIV	Yes	Yes	Yes
Colombia	COL	Yes	Yes	Yes
Costa Rica	CRI	Yes	Yes	Yes
Cyprus	CYP	Yes	Yes	Yes
Czechia	CZE	Yes	Yes	Yes
Germany	DEU	Yes	Yes	Yes
Denmark	DNK	Yes	Yes	Yes
Dominican Republic	DOM	Yes	Yes	Yes
Ecuador	ECU	Yes	Yes	Yes
Egypt	EGY	Yes	Yes	Yes
Spain	ESP	Yes	Yes	Yes
Estonia	EST	Yes	Yes	Yes
Ethiopia	ETH	Yes	Yes	Yes
Finland	FIN	Yes	Yes	Yes
France	FRA	Yes	Yes	Yes
United Kingdom	GBR	Yes	Yes	Yes
Ghana	GHA	Yes	Yes	Yes
Greece	GRC	Yes	Yes	Yes
Guatemala	GTM	Yes	Yes	Yes
Croatia	HRV			Yes
Hungary	HUN	Yes	Yes	Yes
Indonesia	IDN	Yes	Yes	Yes
India	IND	Yes	Yes	Yes
Ireland	IRL	Yes	Yes	Yes
Iceland	ISL	Yes	Yes	Yes
Israel	ISR	Yes	Yes	Yes
Italy	ITA	Yes	Yes	Yes
Jamaica	JAM	Yes	Yes	Yes
Japan	JPN	Yes	Yes	Yes
Kazakhstan	KAZ		Yes	Yes
Kenya	KEN	Yes	Yes	Yes
Kyrgyzstan	KGZ	Yes	Yes	Yes
Korea	KOR	Yes	Yes	Yes
Sri Lanka	LKA	Yes	Yes	Yes
Lithuania	LTU	Yes	Yes	Yes
Luxembourg	LUX	Yes	Yes	Yes
Latvia	LVA	Yes	Yes	Yes

Country	ISO alpha-3 code	2018	2021	2023
Morocco	MAR	Yes	Yes	Yes
Madagascar	MDG	Yes	Yes	Yes
Mexico	MEX	Yes	Yes	Yes
Malta	MLT			Yes
Mauritius	MUS			Yes
Malaysia	MYS	Yes	Yes	Yes
Nigeria	NGA	Yes	Yes	Yes
Netherlands	NLD	Yes	Yes	Yes
Norway	NOR	Yes	Yes	Yes
New Zealand	NZL	Yes	Yes	Yes
Panama	PAN	Yes	Yes	Yes
Peru	PER	Yes	Yes	Yes
Philippines	PHL	Yes	Yes	Yes
Poland	POL	Yes	Yes	Yes
Portugal	PRT	Yes	Yes	Yes
Paraguay	PRY	Yes	Yes	Yes
Romania	ROU			Yes
Russia	RUS	Yes	Yes	Yes
Rwanda	RWA	Yes	Yes	Yes
Singapore	SGP			Yes
Slovak Republic	SVK	Yes	Yes	Yes
Slovenia	SVN	Yes	Yes	Yes
Sweden	SWE	Yes	Yes	Yes
Türkiye	TUR	Yes	Yes	Yes
Uganda	UGA	Yes	Yes	Yes
Ukraine	UKR	Yes	Yes	Yes
Uruguay	URY	Yes	Yes	Yes
United States	USA	Yes	Yes	Yes
South Africa	ZAF	Yes	Yes	Yes
Zambia	ZMB			Yes

Source: Authors.

Table A.3. World Bank Country Classification

Low income economies	Lower-middle-income economies	Upper-middle-income economies	High income economies
Burkina Faso (BFA)	Bangladesh (BGD)	Argentina (ARG)	Australia (AUS)
Ethiopia (ETH)	Côte d'Ivoire (CIV)	Bulgaria (BGR)	Austria (AUT)
Madagascar (MDG)	Egypt (EGY)	Brazil (BRA)	Belgium (BEL)
Rwanda (RWA)	Ghana (GHA)	China (CHN)	Canada (CAN)
Uganda (UGA)	India (IND)	Colombia (COL)	Switzerland (CHE)
	Kenya (KEN)	Costa Rica (CRI)	Chile (CHL)
	Kyrgyztan (KGZ)	Dominican Rep. (DOM)	Cyprus (CYP)
	Sri Lanka (LKA)	Ecuador (ECU)	Czechia (CZE)
	Morocco (MAR)	Guatemala (GTM)	Germany (DEU)
	Nigeria (NGA)	Indonesia (IDN)	Denmark (DNK)
	the Philippines (PHL)	Jamaica (JAM)	Spain (ESP)
	Ukraine (UKR)	Kazahkstan (KAZ)	Estonia (EST)
	Zambia (ZMB)	Mexico (MEX)	Finland (FIN)
		Mauritius (MUS)	France (FRA)
		Malaysia (MYS)	United Kingdom (GBR)
		Peru (PER)	Greece (GRC)
		Paraguay (PRY)	Croatia (HRV)
		Russia (RUS)	Hungary (HUN)
		South Africa (ZAF)	Ireland (IRL)
			Iceland (ISL)
			Israel (ISR)
			Italy (ITA)
			Japan (JPN)
			Korea (KOR)
			Lithuania (LTU)
			Luxembourg (LUX)
			Latvia (LVA)
			Malta (MLT)
			the Netherlands (NLD)
			Norway (NOR)
			New Zealand (NZL)
			Panama (PAN)
			Poland (POL)
			Portugal (PRT)
			Romania (ROU)
			Singapore (SGP)
			Slovakia (SVK)

Source: World Bank Country and Lending Groups 2024